THE COUNTRYSIDE
OF APHRODISIAS

THE **COUNTRYSIDE** OF **APHRODISIAS**

CHRISTOPHER RATTÉ AND ANGELA COMMITO

CONTRIBUTIONS BY
Örgü Dalgıç, Peter De Staebler, Ian Lockey,
Leah Long, Felipe Rojas, and Heather Turnbow

Kelsey Museum Publication 15
Ann Arbor, Michigan 2017

KELSEY MUSEUM PUBLICATIONS

The Kelsey Museum of Archaeology at the University of Michigan supports teaching and research on Mediterranean, Egyptian, and Near Eastern archaeology through stewardship of its rich collections, an active exhibitions program, and sponsorship of ongoing field research. The Kelsey Museum also has an active publications program, including the Kelsey Museum Fieldwork Series, which produces academic reports on Kelsey-sponsored field projects, and the Kelsey Museum Publication series, which has traditionally focused on exhibition catalogues. The present volume inaugurates a new type of publication within the Kelsey Museum Publication Series, namely, short monographs on field projects sponsored in whole or in part by the Kelsey Museum, intended for the general public. This book is being published simultaneously in English and Turkish, and it is hoped that future publications in this series will also appear both in English and in the languages of the countries where our teams work. In this way, we hope to pay back a small part of the debt we owe our host countries, as well as to share the results of our work with a broader international public.

Published by:
Kelsey Museum of Archaeology
434 South State Street
Ann Arbor, Michigan 48109-1390

© Kelsey Museum of Archaeology 2017

ISBN 978-0-9906623-5-8

CONTENTS

PREFACE

A systematic program of archaeological research at the Greek and Roman city of Aphrodisias in southwestern Turkey was begun in 1961. This program has focused on large-scale excavation of the central monuments of Aphrodisias, a prosperous town of around 10,000 inhabitants, with spectacular results. Well-preserved marble buildings, including the Temple of Aphrodite and the Theater together with other public monuments such as honorific inscriptions and portrait statues, combine to bring the civic culture of Aphrodisias and the ancient Mediterranean world vividly to life.

Until recently, however, modern knowledge of ancient Aphrodisias extended only as far as the city's fortification walls. Very little attention had been paid to the monuments outside the gates—beginning with the suburban roads and cemeteries—or to the study of the relationship between the urban settlement and its rural environs. Although the excavations had revealed one of the world's best-preserved ancient cities, important questions about the history of the city remained unanswered.

It is a truism of Classical studies that in the Greek and Roman periods a city and its territory formed an inseparable unit, which the Greeks called a *polis*. Cities were dependent on the natural environment for water and food, as well as other resources, such as, in the case of Aphrodisias, the marble that made its architects and sculptors famous. Obvious subjects of local interest at Aphrodisias were the water supply, the nature of agricultural exploitation of the valley, and the local geology. Where were the springs and the aqueducts? What were the major crops? Where did the marble come from?

Throughout most of human history, moreover, the inhabitants of this valley have not lived in a single city but rather in villages and isolated farmsteads scattered throughout the surrounding countryside. To understand how the ancient city came into being—what settlement in the region looked like before the city was founded in the second century BC—it was necessary to look outside the City Wall. To understand the circumstances of the city's near abandonment in the seventh century AD, it was also necessary to adopt a larger frame of reference, to determine, for example, whether the depopulation of the city was due to an increase in mortality or simply to a change in settlement pattern.

These are among the research questions that lay behind the archaeological survey of the region around Aphrodisias carried out between 2005 and 2009. This five-year program of interdisciplinary research brought together archaeologists, art historians, natural scientists, and geographers in order to investigate the relationship between human habitation and the natural environment at and around Aphrodisias from the prehistoric period to the present day, with a special focus on the heyday of the city in the Hellenistic and Roman periods (second century BC to seventh century AD). A multi-authored academic report edited by Christopher Ratté and Peter D. De Staebler on the results of the survey appeared in 2012.[1] The present volume condenses the fieldwork and research of the survey team into a revised and abridged version of the academic publication. It presents our findings in a more accessible format, which we hope will be of interest both to general readers and to visitors to Aphrodisias curious about the city's surroundings.

The research presented here would not have been possible without the support and encouragement of numerous individuals and institutions. Our first debt of thanks is owed to the General Directorate of Cultural Resources and Museums of the Ministry of Culture and Tourism of the Republic of Turkey, for permission to undertake the Aphrodisias Regional Survey and for invaluable assistance of all kinds. We are particularly grateful to the government representatives assigned to our project for each field season, who did a great deal in large ways and small to facilitate our work: Akan Atila (2005), Erman Bedioğlu (2006), Musa Tombul (2007), Mustafa Akaslan (2008), and Çağman Esirgemez (2009). Research at Aphrodisias and environs is sponsored by the Institute of Fine Arts and the Faculty of Arts and Science at New York University, and we would like to thank James

R. McCredie, Mariët Westermann, Michèle Marincola, and Patricia Rubin, recent and current directors of the Institute of Fine Arts, for their support. The project director of the Aphrodisias excavations is Professor R. R. R. Smith, whose collegial interest is deeply appreciated, and who read and very helpfully commented on earlier versions of this volume. Peter De Staebler was Assistant Director of the Aphrodisias Regional Survey, and this book owes a great deal to his efforts as co-editor of the academic report on which it is based.

The principal financial supporter of the project was the Leon Levy Foundation, and we are profoundly grateful for the interest and commitment of the officers of the Foundation. From 2007 to 2009, the project was also supported by various units of the University of Michigan, including the Department of Classical Studies; the Kelsey Museum of Archaeology; the Map Library; the College of Literature, Science, and the Arts; the Rackham Graduate School; and the Office of the Vice President for Research, all of which we gratefully acknowledge. We are also indebted to the Geyre Foundation, the Joukowsky Family Foundation, and the American Research Institute in Turkey for generous moral and financial support.

For the production of the maps, drawings, and photographs, we would like to express our particular debt to our GIS team, Jaime Martinez, Jamieson Donati, Anastasia Kuznetsov, Christopher Harrison, Ryan Hughes, and Jana Mokrišová; to our architectural staff, Emily Corbett, Harry Mark, Erin Putalik, and Felipe Rojas; to the Kelsey Museum's graphic artist, Lorene Sterner; and to our photographer, Benjamin Swett. It also gives us great pleasure to thank the Aphrodisias excavation's restoration architects, Thomas Kaefer and Gerhard Paul, and the former project coordinator, Orhan Atvur, for their friendship and logistical support. For the design and implementation of the electronic publication of our results, we are very grateful to Jim Ottaviani of the University of Michigan Library. For copyediting and book design, we are indebted to Margaret Lourie.

Last but not least, we would like to express our gratitude to the people of the region around Aphrodisias: our friends in Geyre, especially Cihat

Members of Aphrodisias staff
(2005): Nami Çoban, Metin
Dağ, Veysel Dağ, and Cihat
Çoban.

Çoban, Nami Çoban, Veysel Dağ, and Metin Dağ (photo above); the
mayors and imams of the villages we visited; archaeologist Mahir Atıcı,
a native of Karacasu; and above all, the shepherds, on whose incompara-
ble knowledge of the local topography we continually relied. To them, the
most important custodians of the region's cultural heritage, we owe a very
special debt of thanks.

CHRONOLOGY

The following chronological categories are used in this book:

Prehistoric: before ca. 1000 BC

Pre-Hellenistic: ca. 1000 BC to late fourth century BC
Iron Age: ca. 1000–600 BC
Archaic: sixth to early fifth century BC
Classical: early fifth to late fourth century BC

Hellenistic/Augustan: late fourth century BC to early first century AD
Early Hellenistic: late fourth to second century BC
Late Hellenistic/Augustan: second century BC to early first century AD

Roman Imperial: early first to late fourth century AD
Early Imperial: first century AD
High Imperial: second to early third century AD
Late Roman: early third to late fourth century AD

Late Antique: late fourth to mid-seventh century AD

Medieval, or Middle Ages: mid-seventh to 11th century AD
Early Byzantine ("Dark Age"): mid-seventh to eighth century AD
Middle Byzantine: ninth to 11th century AD

Early Turkish (Seljuk): 11th to 15th century AD

Ottoman: 15th century AD to 1922

Modern Turkish (Republican): 1922 to present

Fig. 1.1. Map of Western Asia Minor.

1 INTRODUCTION

Topography

The ancient city of Aphrodisias lies in the Maeander River basin, about 150 km east of the Aegean coast of Turkey (fig. 1.1). It is located in the ancient region of Caria, on the south side of the Maeander, in the fertile valley of a tributary stream called the Morsynus (the modern Dandalas). The valley of the Morsynus divides naturally into two roughly equal parts: the lower valley, on the edge of the Maeander plain, and the upper valley, near the river's source. Aphrodisias is situated at the center of the upper valley, 35 km up the Morsynus from its confluence with the Maeander, at an elevation of ca. 500 masl.

The region of the upper Morsynus River valley was the major focus of the Aphrodisias survey (see front flap). This region encompasses an area of approximately 475 km², ranging in elevation from 350 masl at the west end of the valley to 2,300 masl at the summit of Mount Kadmos (Baba Dağı), the source of the Morsynus, to the east (figs. 1.2–5). Its principal natural

Fig. 1.2. View of countryside from Theater at Aphrodisias, looking east.

Fig. 1.3. View of Aphrodisias survey region from Baba Dağı, looking southwest.

Fig. 1.4. Aerial view of Aphrodisias, looking southeast (photograph by Jonathan Blair, reproduced with permission of the National Geographic Society).

Fig. 1.5. Summit of Baba Dağı, looking south-east.

Fig. 1.6. Morsynus River near Karacasu, looking northwest.

resources are the abundant springs of the surrounding mountains and the fertile soils of the valley floor; other notable assets include potter's earth and marble, both still actively quarried today (figs. 1.6–8). The major modern settlement in the area is the market town of Karacasu, which lies at the western edge of the survey area. In addition to the valley proper, the survey area included the adjoining plateau to the southwest (approximately 200 km²), which epigraphic and archaeological evidence (discussed below) had indicated belonged to the territory of Aphrodisias in the Hellenistic and Roman periods, and part of the valley of the Timeles River (also referred to as the plain of Tabae) to the southeast (approximately 125 km²), which was the source of one of Roman Aphrodisias's major aqueducts (figs. 1.9–10).

Fig. 1.7. Karacasu pottery district.

Fig. 1.8. Modern marble quarries of Demirağlar Marble Industry & Trade Ltd., looking southeast.

Fig. 1.9. View of southwest plateau from lower slopes of Karıncalı Dağı, looking south.

Fig. 1.10. Kepiz Çayı, a tributary of the Timeles River.

Ancient Sources for the Region around Aphrodisias

Ancient sources for the topography of the region around Aphrodisias are limited. From the writings of ancient geographers and lexicographers we know the names of Antioch on the Maeander (modern Başaran), at the confluence of the Morsynus and Maeander Rivers; of Aphrodisias itself; and of Tabae (modern Kale), the principal city of the fertile plain to the southeast of the Morsynus River basin. The major rivers of the region are the Morsynus, most usefully described by the Roman historian Pliny as the river that together with the Maeander "flows around" Antioch,[2] and the Timeles, attested only in coins, inscriptions, and a marble relief. The Timeles was convincingly identified by the French epigraphers Louis and Jeanne Robert as the modern Yenidere, the river that drains the plain of Tabae into the Harpasus (modern Akçay), the next major tributary of the Maeander west of the Morsynus.[3] The dominant feature of the landscape of the region is Baba Dağı, persuasively identified by the Roberts as ancient Mount Kadmos.[4] The meanings of the names of both the mountain and the rivers remain unclear.

The most important historical text for the geography of the region is the Roman historian Livy's account of the upland march of Gnaeus Manlius Vulso, a Roman general, in his campaign against the Gauls in 189 BC. Livy describes the progress of Manlius's army from Antioch on the Maeander to Tabae: "From there [Antioch] they proceeded to a place

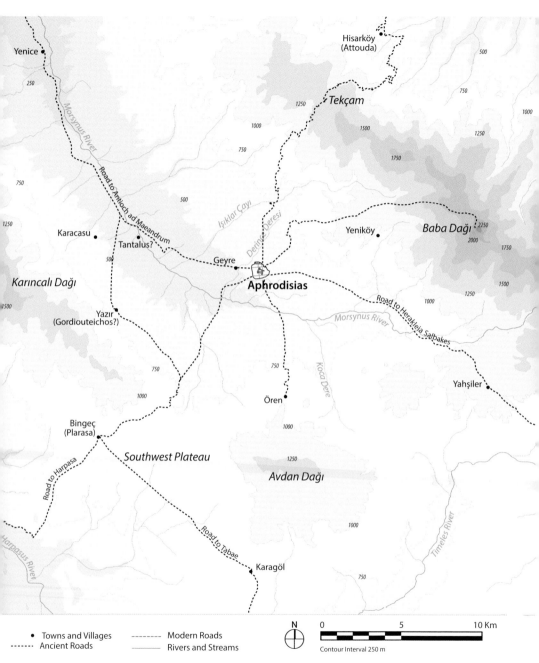

Fig. 1.11. Map of Aphrodisias survey region, showing possible routes of ancient roads.

Fig. 1.12. Possible site
of Byzantine citadel of
Tantalus, looking west.

called Gordiouteichos. From that place, they reached Tabae after three days'
march."[5] The distance from Antioch to Tabae is 55 km as the crow flies. The
most direct route would take a traveler straight up the lower Morsynus valley, along the south side of the upper Morsynus valley south of Aphrodisias,
over the low mountain at the southeast corner of the valley (Avdan Dağı),
and then across the Timeles River to Tabae (fig. 1.11). A chain of modern
roads that circumvents Avdan Dağı to the southwest hews closely to this
route. Livy's account implies that Gordiouteichos, also mentioned in an
inscription from Aphrodisias[6] and attested by its own coinage,[7] lay within
a day's march of Antioch, and that Tabae lay within three days' march of
Gordiouteichos. Approximately one-third of the way from Antioch (20 km
as the crow flies) lies the modern village of Yazır, and an ancient citadel on
the slopes above Yazır may have been associated with Gordiouteichos.

A much later reference to another army passing through the Morsynus
River valley is the account by the Byzantine historian Nicetas Choniates
of the campaign of the Sultan of Iconium, Kaykhusraw I, against Antioch
on the Maeander.[8] On the way to Antioch (moving from east to west),
Kaykhusraw first attacked a place called Caria, apparently the Medieval
name of Aphrodisias, and then Tantalus, probably situated near a modern
hamlet at the west edge of the upper Morsynus valley called Dandalas,
where a substantial Byzantine citadel is located (fig. 1.12).[9] Both places

were captured and their populations deported to Philomelium, modern Akşehir, 250 km away.

Apart from these two references, which bracket the history of Aphrodisias as an ancient and Medieval town, and from the evidence of archaeology, our principal sources of information for the historical geography of Aphrodisias and environs are inscriptions, mainly from Aphrodisias itself, and coins. In the earliest documents (both inscriptions and coins), Aphrodisias is always mentioned in combination with another place called Plarasa, apparently as the junior partner in a union known as "the city or people of the Plarasans and Aphrodisians." The wording implies the two communities were originally independent and were later joined in what the Greeks called a *synoikism* or *sympolity*.[10] Plarasa, named first, seems originally to have been the greater of the two entities. By the late first century BC, however, it had been eclipsed by Aphrodisias, and its name dropped out of currency. Most scholars have identified Plarasa with the modern village of Bingeç on the plateau southwest of Aphrodisias, and the results of our research support that contention. Bingeç is the only other site in the region besides Aphrodisias itself with a large cemetery, and it is the only other site to have produced a significant number of inscriptions, of which one refers to Plarasa and Aphrodisias. It is interesting that apparently the most important early urban settlement in the region was located in the more remote area of the southwest plateau rather than in the more fertile, but also more vulnerable, Morsynus River valley.

Progress of Research and Survey Methodology

Fieldwork for the Aphrodisias Regional Survey was begun in 2005 and completed in 2009. The purpose of the first season was to conduct a preliminary three-week reconnaissance of the survey area with a relatively small team of eight persons. In 2006–2008 the season was lengthened to six weeks and the team enlarged to 14 persons on average. The 2009 season was limited to fact-checking and reexamination of finds by three persons for 10 days.

Our field research combined "extensive" and "intensive" approaches to archaeological survey. The extensive survey involved visits to all the towns

Fig. 1.13. Field-walkers collecting pottery and other surface finds during intensive transect survey.

and villages in the survey area; interviews with local shepherds, farmers, and officials such as village mayors, school teachers, and imams; and detailed recording of archaeological points of interest shown to us by these informants (including controlled collection of surface finds, graphic and photographic recording, and incorporation into a GIS, or Geographical Information System). Intensive survey involved field-by-field examination of an area extending 500 m in every direction outside the city walls of Aphrodisias and survey of a series of "transects"—strips 5 km long and 50 m wide—radiating out of the center of the city (fig. 1.13). The extensive survey has provided us with a reasonably complete inventory of known archaeological sites in the survey region, the vast majority of which, while familiar to the local population, were completely unknown to the archaeological community. At the same time, the intensive survey, following established sampling procedures and data-collection methods, gave us a more systematically assembled dataset for the central part of the region. By combining these two sources of information, which yielded a total of approximately 670 archaeological points of interest, we can reconstruct a detailed picture of the history of human settlement and the exploitation of natural resources in the area around Aphrodisias from the mid-first millennium BC to the Middle Ages.

2 BEFORE THE FOUNDING OF APHRODISIAS

Prehistoric

Although stray finds suggest human habitation at Aphrodisias as early as the Late Neolithic (late sixth millennium BC), the earliest intensive occupation of the site has been dated to the Late Chalcolithic period (mid–late fifth millennium BC). At this time, a small agricultural settlement was established on two low mounds: the Pekmez and Theater hills (fig. 2.1). Excavations carried out in the late 1960s and early 1970s unearthed a long sequence of occupation layers.[11] Of special interest is the Early Bronze Age (third millennium BC), represented by the remains of mudbrick houses and pithos burials, by a pottery assemblage attesting relations both with the Aegean coast and with sites farther to the east, such as Beycesultan, and by notable artifacts including a large number of small figurines in marble and other stones. Later prehistoric periods are less well represented, but with some short gaps, occupation has been continuous until the present day.

The Aphrodisias Regional Survey recorded little evidence for human presence in the surrounding countryside before the mid-first millennium BC. In particular, we found no prehistoric settlement mounds outside Aphrodisias, and it seems unlikely that any such mounds would have been eroded away or covered up or would have entirely escaped the notice of the contemporary inhabitants. However, two substantial prehistoric mounds are known on the plain of Tabae to the southeast, at the modern villages of Karahisar and Medet (Apollonia Salbakes). A network of prehistoric settlements can therefore be traced across the Morsynus River valley and the plain to the southeast. One additional site of interest in the Aphrodisias region is a large cave (450 m deep) on the south side of the valley near the village of Çamarası (see chapter 7). Ceramic and tile fragments were found in the cave at distances of up to 100 m from the entrance, including pottery tentatively dated to the Middle and Late Bronze Ages (second millennium BC).[12]

Fig. 2.1. Theater hill (prehistoric mound), looking southeast.

Mid- and Late First Millennium BC

After an apparent gap of several centuries at the end of the second millennium BC, occupation at the "acropolis" mound (Theater hill) at Aphrodisias becomes visible again in or before the sixth century BC. In this period, the region around Aphrodisias was dominated by the kingdom of Lydia, centered in the valley of the Hermus (modern Gediz) River to the north (see fig. 1.1), and Lydian imports are indeed the most diagnostic Iron Age pottery finds from the acropolis. The pottery was found in association with rubble walls and graves suggestive of a small settlement. Imported Lydian and Greek pottery of sixth-century date is also found at Aphrodisias in the area of the later Temple of Aphrodite. The pottery from this area is distinctly finer than that from the acropolis, and the establishment of the sanctuary as such likely dates to or before this period.[13] At least as early as the sixth century, therefore, Aphrodisias seems to have taken form as a local cult center associated with a small permanent settlement. Stray finds of grave stelai, statues of lions, and two fragmentary Lydian inscriptions all probably come from grave monuments of the sixth to fourth centuries BC.[14] Outside Aphrodisias, the most dramatic evidence for pre-Hellenistic and Early Hellenistic occupation consists of a number of burial

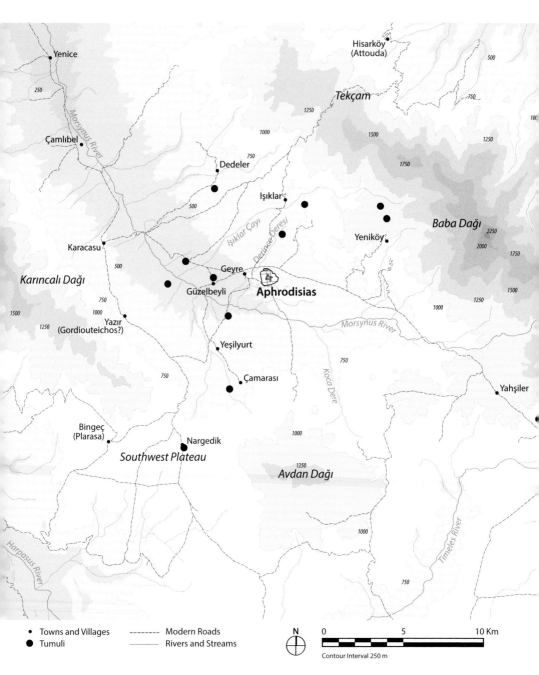

Fig. 2.2. Map of Aphrodisias survey region, showing locations of tumuli.

Fig. 2.3. Yertepe (Güzel-beyli tumulus), looking east.

mounds, or tumuli, several of which mark the locations of built chamber tombs, and a series of isolated fortified citadels and watchtowers found on both the north and south sides of the Morsynus valley.

Tumuli

The tumuli give the best evidence for the social organization and cultural identity of the occupants of the region before the establishment of a Greek city at Aphrodisias in or before the late second century BC. A total of 12 certain or probable tumulus tombs have been identified in the survey region (not including the necropolis of Plarasa), and at least two further tumuli are attested in the lower Morsynus valley, outside the survey region, at the villages of Çamlıbel and Yenice (fig. 2.2). The tombs are widely dispersed over a variety of different geographical situations on both sides of the valley floor as well as in the hills to the north and south. The distribution of these monumental graves seems to reflect a pre-urban society in which the valley was dominated by an aristocracy of large landowners—possibly buried either on their rural estates (the tumulus tombs close to the river) or next to their dependent villages (the tumulus tombs in the hills north of the river).

The majority of the tumuli are relatively small, approximately 20–25 m in preserved diameter and about 5 m high (fig. 2.3). Most of the tombs have no external features beyond the earthen mound, but one exceptional

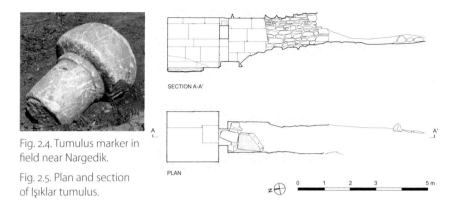

SECTION A-A'

PLAN

Fig. 2.4. Tumulus marker in field near Nargedik.

Fig. 2.5. Plan and section of Işıklar tumulus.

tumulus, in the hills above Yeniköy (the northernmost of the two tumuli north of Yeniköy; see fig. 2.2), was bordered at the base by a low stone wall. In addition, two limestone "phallus markers" have been found in the region: one in the dromos of the tumulus at Çamlıbel, the other on the north edge of the southwest plateau, on the edge of the village of Nargedik (figs. 2.2 and 2.4). Markers of this type are in fact unlikely to have been phalloi but are rather round knobs on stems that were inserted into the tops of the mounds.

Where exposed, the tomb chambers buried beneath the mounds are either rock-cut or built out of ashlar masonry (i.e., out of large squared blocks) in a variety of stones, including marble, sandstone, conglomerate, and schist. The most elaborate of the chamber complexes (3 km north of Aphrodisias, on the east side of the Derince Deresi between Aphrodisias and Işıklar; see fig. 2.2) consists of an oblong chamber with a flat ceiling (H: 1.85 m; W: 1.88 m; L: 2.04 m), entered by way of a slightly smaller antechamber, built like the chamber of ashlar masonry; the antechamber is in turn approached by a dromos or corridor-like passageway at least 6 m long, bordered by carefully constructed rubble walls (figs. 2.5–6). When first recorded, two simple freestanding funerary couches, or *klinai*, were set up along the side walls of the chamber. A doorway centered in the front wall of the chamber was closed by a fitted doorplug. Other tomb chambers are comparable in size, and several have an antechamber but no dromos.

Fig. 2.6. View looking north down dromos of Işıklar tumulus.

In place of *klinai*, some tomb chambers (e.g., the chamber of the tumulus north of Yeşilyurt; see fig. 2.2) have schist slabs slotted into the back and one side of the chamber, in which case the door in the front wall is not centered but shifted to one side; this may represent a specific local burial tradition (figs. 2.7–8). In addition, the ceiling of an exceptional chamber on the west edge of the plain of Tabae southeast of Yahşiler (see fig. 2.2) is supported by two evenly spaced transverse beams—another local tradition best represented by the tumuli of the Harpasus River valley (fig. 2.9).

Lydia provides the closest parallels for tomb chambers and tumuli of the types found in the area around Aphrodisias. As noted above, Lydia was an independent kingdom that dominated neighboring regions from the late seventh through the mid-sixth century, when it was conquered by Persia, inaugurating a period of Persian rule throughout Asia Minor that extended from the 540s BC until the coming of Alexander the Great in 334 BC. The earliest tumuli with stone burial chambers in Lydia date to the early sixth century BC, and the tradition continued through the Persian period. The tomb chambers and tumuli around Aphrodisias seem to document the acculturation of the local élite to Lydian cultural norms, and so may be dated to roughly the same period. In later times, Aphrodisias belonged to Caria, but it is important to note that the site actually lies in a natural frontier region, at the east end of the Maeander River basin, near the borders of ancient Caria, Lydia, and Phrygia. Elements of all three

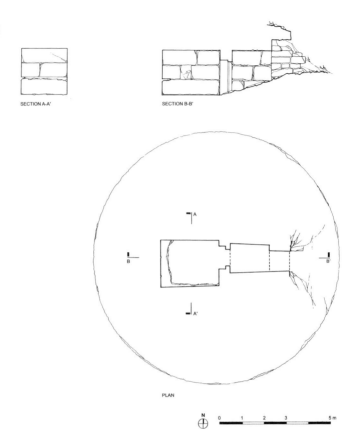

Fig. 2.7. Plan and section of Yeşilyurt tumulus.

SECTION A-A'

SECTION B-B'

PLAN

N

0   1   2   3   5 m

Fig. 2.8. Interior of Yeşilyurt tumulus, looking west at broken schist slabs slotted into back of chamber.

Anatolian traditions as well, of course, as those of Greece and Rome can be found in the later culture of the city. Before the sixth century BC, however, it is unclear that the local population conformed to any clearly defined ethnic category—for example, that they spoke any of the languages that we can identify epigraphically rather than a separate nonliterary dialect. In general terms, the initial expansion of the Lydian kingdom followed by the unification of Asia Minor under Persian rule could be said to have stimulated the local élite in the region around Aphrodisias to enlarge on its purely local identity by adopting some of the

Fig. 2.9. Interior of Yahşiler tumulus, looking west-northwest at corner of chamber.

practices of the dominant regional culture of Lydia—as seen not only in the tumulus tombs throughout the region but also in the appearance of imported Lydian pottery and Lydian inscriptions at Aphrodisias itself. The tumuli in particular also seem to indicate the presence of a landed aristocracy since most of these tombs would appear to mark local estates, although several mounds that lie near settlements, occupied in the Hellenistic period if not earlier, in the hills on the north side of the valley may have been associated with dependent villages. These changes do not necessarily imply the movement of a new élite population of Lydian origin into the region; neither should we feel obliged to read into the adoption of Lydian cultural practices by the local élite any necessary conflict between élite and non-élite populations—but rather the creation of a typically complex, hybrid local culture.

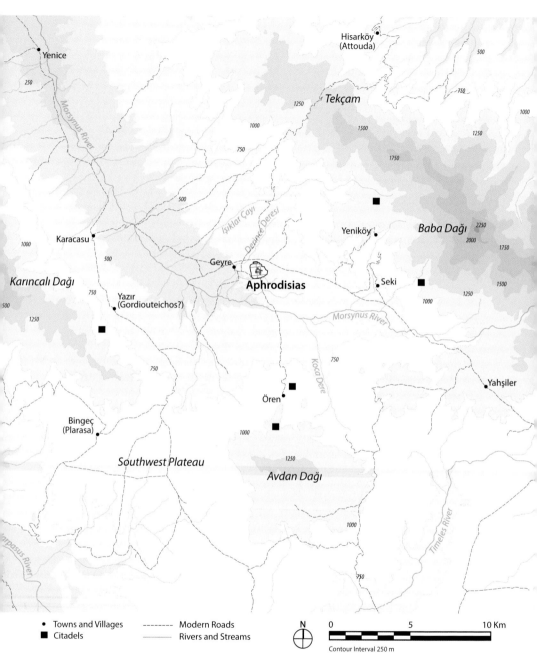

Fig. 2.10. Map of Aphrodisias survey region, showing locations of pre-Roman citadels and watchtowers.

Territorial Fortifications

After tumuli and other tombs, the next category of monumental archaeological evidence for pre- and Early Hellenistic activity in the region around Aphrodisias is a loose network of fortified citadels and watchtowers (fig. 2.10). On the south side of the Morsynus River valley, these include a small fortified citadel near modern Yazır and two isolated watchtowers in the vicinity of the modern village of Ören. On the north side of the valley are a similar small fortified citadel near modern Seki and a larger fortified enclosure near modern Yeniköy. All these structures have certain architectural characteristics in common, such as towers built of isodomic or roughly isodomic masonry (i.e., ashlar masonry with courses of equal height) and drafted corners (a masonry technique in which the faces of the blocks are roughly dressed except at the corners of towers, which are defined by smoothly dressed vertical bands, meeting at right angles to form a salient corner; see fig. 2.13). All are built of materials readily available in the immediate surroundings, including schist, marble, and blue-gray limestone. In addition, all the fortifications are strategically located near or in view of major roads: from the Morsynus River valley to the southwest plateau (Yazır and Ören), from the valley to the southeast plain of Tabae (Seki), or from the Morsynus River valley via the Baba Dağı Ridge to the valleys of the Maeander and Lycus Rivers (Yeniköy). On the combined evidence of architectural characteristics and surface pottery, they may all be roughly dated to the fourth to second centuries BC.

The fortified citadel near Yazır (elevation 980–995 masl) sits atop a promontory-like hill that crowns a ridge running down toward the modern village and commands a sweeping view over the valley below (figs. 2.10–12). The modern name of the citadel is Gâvur Pazaryeri, or Marketplace of the Infidel. It has been associated with the town of Gordiouteichos, which, while it had become a Greek city by the time it issued coins in the Late Hellenistic period, may also have its origins in the stronghold of a local potentate, as the "fortress of Gordis." As preserved, the citadel has three main components. In the center at the top of the hill is a large rectangular two-chambered tower, 8.49 m wide and 13.13 m long, built mostly out of neatly dressed schist blocks.

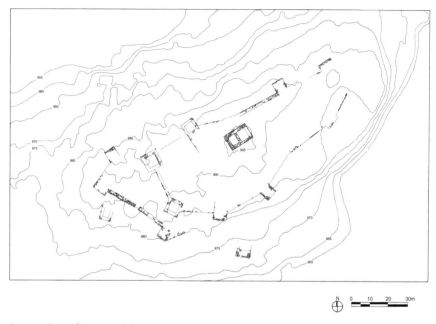

Fig. 2.11. Plan of Yazır citadel.

A notable feature of the masonry is the careful drafting of the exterior corners, especially visible on the southwest corner (fig. 2.13). This central tower,
or keep, lies within a fortified area of ca. 4,000 m², enclosed by a curtain wall
1.5 m thick and punctuated by six or more towers. Like the keep, the curtain
wall and associated towers are largely built out of schist, except for the relatively well-preserved towers on the southwest side, flanking what seems to
have been the main or sole entryway into the fortified area. The towers on
either side of this entranceway are built out of neatly squared marble blocks
laid in roughly isodomic courses, with drafting similar to that of the keep at
the exterior corners. The third component of the citadel is an outer wall on
the southwest side, apparently independent of the main part of the citadel
and very different in appearance from the curtain wall; this outer wall may
in fact have been a later addition to the citadel. It is built partly of marble,
partly of schist, with towers at both ends and a doorway in the center, 2.6 m
wide with its marble threshold still in situ. A third tower lies to the north of

Fig. 2.12. Reconstruction of Yazır citadel, looking northeast.

Fig. 2.13. Drafted southwest corner of central tower of Yazır citadel, looking northeast.

the northwestern tower and is connected with it. No connection with the main part of the citadel is preserved. There are also at least two apparently freestanding towers or structures to the south of the citadel.

Two isolated watchtowers are located in the vicinity of Ören: one on a hill 0.75 km north of the village, the other in the foothills of Avdan Dağı, 1.75 km south of the village (see fig. 2.10). The better-preserved southern watchtower is 7.4 m wide and appears to be 7.8 m long, with walls built out of white and blue-gray marble (figs. 2.14–15). The masonry of the exterior

Fig. 2.14. Plan of watchtower south of Ören.

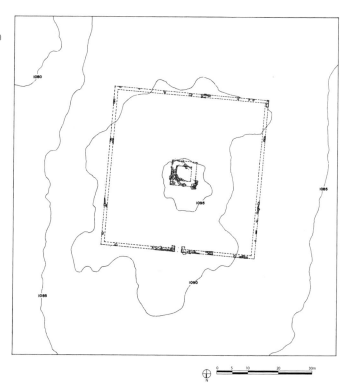

Fig. 2.15. Front (north side) of watchtower south of Ören, looking south.

face is laid in trapezoidal fashion, and the corners are drafted. The tower is surrounded by a square enclosure wall of schist and quartz, 48 m long on a side (so enclosing an area of approximately 2,300 m²), with an opening 2.15 m wide centered on the south side. The watchtower north of Ören, 6.5 m by 6.4 m, is also constructed of marble blocks and appears to be surrounded by a rectangular enclosure wall.

The small fortified citadel east of the modern village of Seki is dramatically situated on steep bluffs that rise to elevations of 1,100–1,120 masl above the east bank of a streambed known locally as Kale Deresi, or Castle Stream (figs. 2.10, 2.16–17). The main part of the citadel occupies the summit of the bluff. On the north and northwest sides, the cliffs fall away in a vertical drop of over 50 m. The fortified area of ca. 4,500 m² is roughly rectangular and is enclosed by a curtain wall built largely of regularly coursed blocks of schist conglomerate, with occasional blocks of fine blue-gray limestone. The northwest corner of the enclosure is cut off by the line of the cliff. The southeast side of the curtain wall is punctuated by a blocked gate, 2.64 m wide, flanked by two towers. Each tower projects through the curtain wall and is slightly trapezoidal in shape, 6.8 m wide on the interior, 7.9 m wide on the exterior, and 6.7 m deep, with doorways on the sides facing into the enclosed area. Two additional towers are located at the south corner; they are smaller than the towers flanking the gate and abut on, rather than project through, the curtain wall. A second, smaller opening occurs at the west end of the southwest wall, just before the edge of the cliff. A number of structures within the citadel are partially preserved at foundation level: a series of rooms at the northeast corner of the citadel, a possible central tower supported by a substantial terrace wall, and several smaller walls in the southwest part of the citadel. The main approach to the citadel was from the south, where there are two freestanding towers ca. 70 m downhill from the citadel (fig. 2.18). Presumably the road to the citadel led between these two towers, northward to the south corner of the citadel (also guarded by two towers), and then northeastward to the main gate, or northwestward to the smaller gate.

The citadel north of Yeniköy is located on a hill overlooking a deep gorge that separates the southern foothills of Baba Dağı from the ridge

Fig. 2.16. Plan of Seki citadel.

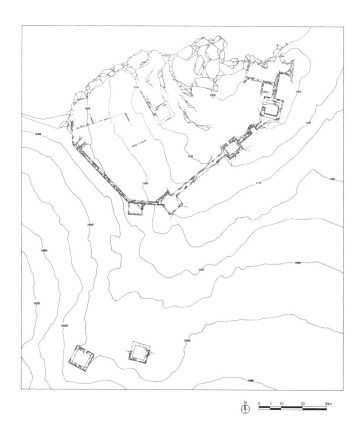

Fig. 2.17. General view toward Seki citadel, on ridge in middle distance, looking north.

Fig. 2.18. Southwest tower of Seki citadel, looking southwest, with view of Morsynus River valley.

Fig. 2.19. North wall of Yeniköy citadel, looking east toward Baba Dağı.

that runs along the north side of the Morsynus River valley (elevation 1,252 masl) (see fig. 2.10). The citadel occupies an area of approximately 3.4 ha (7.5–8.5 times the size of the citadels at Yazır and Seki) and is located near a prominent tumulus tomb articulated by a low stone wall, noted above. To the north, the wall of the citadel runs along the brow of the hill; the fortified area is the gently sloping south side of the hill (fig. 2.19). The walls are built largely of schist with occasional large blocks of quartz and are punctuated by at least 10 towers. The towers are best preserved at the northeast corner; the westerly northeast tower is 4.55 m wide and projects 3.85 m from the curtain wall. The northeast corner of this tower is carefully drafted. The main entrances to the citadel seem to have been to the southeast and northwest. At the southeast corner, there were apparently two large towers, and it seems likely that a road ran between them; this is in fact also the site of a modern tractor path. The northern tower is the more fully preserved and seems to have been about 12 m wide and to have projected at least 10 m in front of the curtain wall. To the northwest, there is another pair of apparent towers at the same elevation as the two towers to the southeast. The modern tractor path is cut through the wall between these two towers, and it is possible that there was an ancient gate nearby. Apart from one north–south wall branching off from the north wall of the citadel, very little evidence survives for construction within the fortified area. It is possibly a *Fluchtburg* on the model of the fortified redoubts in the area around Carian Mylasa, intended to provide a place of refuge for a largely rural population in times of trouble.[15]

In contrast with the tumulus tombs described above, which exhibit close cultural affinities with Lydia, this loosely constituted network of citadels and watchtowers falls squarely within the evolving tradition of Greek military architecture, in terms of both typology and construction technique. As such, it documents a process of increasing integration between western Anatolia and the Greek world, well attested throughout the region—including in Lydia—both in the period of Persian rule and, especially, in the wake of the conquests of Alexander the Great. Broadly speaking, these territorial fortifications may have been built by larger powers, such as the Hecatomnid dynasty (the local rulers who governed the region of Caria on behalf of the Persians) or the Seleucid Empire (the kingdom, formed by one of Alexander's generals, that had established control over all of Asia Minor by the end of the fourth century BC), or by regional entities, such as local aristocrats or nascent urban communities, or by a combination of both. Given the heterogeneous nature and remote locations of the fortifications, the latter alternatives seem more likely, and underscore the complexity and diversity of local culture before the changes of the later Hellenistic period to come.

3 THE FOUNDING OF APHRODISIAS AND ITS IMPACT ON THE SURROUNDING REGION

The next major development in the cultural evolution of the region around Aphrodisias is the establishment of cities on the Greek model. The first clear evidence for this type of community consists of coins and inscriptions of Aphrodisias itself, of Plarasa, and of Gordiouteichos, all datable to the second century BC and subsequent centuries. Recent study of new inscriptions from Aphrodisias has suggested that the city was established as a polis in the immediate aftermath of the treaty known as the Peace of Apamea in 188 BC.[16] This treaty, brokered by Rome, put an effective end to Seleucid control of western Asia Minor and ultimately paved the way for the establishment of the Roman province of Asia in 133 BC. The exact circumstances of the founding of Aphrodisias as a city remain uncertain. In general terms, however, it is clear that the emergence of formally constituted towns in this region was an outgrowth of the intensive urbanization of the neighboring Maeander River valley in the Hellenistic period—whether the primary impetus came from the local population, eager to participate in the benefits that urbanization had brought neighboring communities, or from new settlers, or both.

Aphrodisias had emerged as a local cult center as early as the sixth century BC. As such, it was probably always associated with a small permanent settlement, and when that settlement was formally established as a city in the second century BC, the sanctuary was an obvious source of communal identity. Little is known about the development of the settlement between the sixth and first centuries BC. Presumably the two main focal points of early occupation—the sanctuary area and the acropolis mound (Theater hill)—continued to be occupied throughout the Persian and Hellenistic periods.[17]

The most radical transformation of the urban environment associated with the establishment of the city was the creation of a grid system uniting these two areas (fig. 3.1). The date of the grid plan, which is very similar to

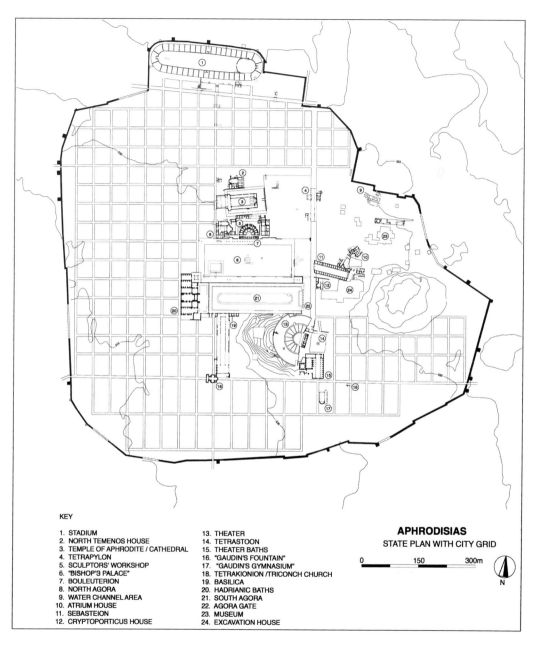

KEY

1. STADIUM
2. NORTH TEMENOS HOUSE
3. TEMPLE OF APHRODITE / CATHEDRAL
4. TETRAPYLON
5. SCULPTORS' WORKSHOP
6. "BISHOP'S PALACE"
7. BOULEUTERION
8. NORTH AGORA
9. WATER CHANNEL AREA
10. ATRIUM HOUSE
11. SEBASTEION
12. CRYPTOPORTICUS HOUSE

13. THEATER
14. TETRASTOON
15. THEATER BATHS
16. "GAUDIN'S FOUNTAIN"
17. "GAUDIN'S GYMNASIUM"
18. TETRAKIONION /TRICONCH CHURCH
19. BASILICA
20. HADRIANIC BATHS
21. SOUTH AGORA
22. AGORA GATE
23. MUSEUM
24. EXCAVATION HOUSE

APHRODISIAS

STATE PLAN WITH CITY GRID

0   150   300m

N

Fig. 3.1. City plan of Aphrodisias.

that of other Late Classical and Hellenistic cities in the Maeander valley region such as Priene and Magnesia, is uncertain.[18] It could be as early as the founding of the city in the early second century BC or as late as the late first century BC, the epigraphically established date of one of the stoas (porticos) of the Agora (the main civic and commercial square), which lies at the heart of the grid. When the city was enclosed by fortification walls in the fourth century AD, encompassing an area of 70 ha, the entire area of the grid was apparently filled with houses, but this is of course unlikely to have been true at the beginning. Nevertheless, it seems clear that a population in the thousands was envisioned at the time the grid was first laid out.

The first century and a half of Aphrodisias's existence as a city was a turbulent period, culminating in the Roman civil wars of the mid-first century BC. Archaeological documentation for this period at Aphrodisias is meager, but the epigraphic record tells us of its disastrous dénouement, when the city was sacked by the renegade Roman general Quintus Labienus in 40 BC.[19] The surrounding territory must also have suffered. In the decade that followed, the city's fortunes took a marked turn for the better, thanks to the connection between Gaius Julius Zoilos, a citizen of Aphrodisias and Roman freedman, and the emerging Roman leader Octavian (later to be given the title of Augustus, as the first Roman emperor). The 30s BC witnessed the beginning of a major program of urban development, focused on the traditional centers of Greek civic life—the Temple of the patron goddess, the large and typically "Ionian" Agora, and the Theater—and perhaps intended in particular to promote the development of the sanctuary of Aphrodite as a regional pilgrimage site (figs. 3.2–3).[20] That the earliest public buildings in the city center date to the late first century BC—as much as a century or more after the founding of the city—is perhaps not surprising. The first structures built in the new town would have been the private houses of its residents, and the uncertain times of the late second and early to mid-first century were hardly conducive to extensive public building. All three of these building projects bear building inscriptions naming Zoilos; all were presumably paid for at least in part with funds provided by Octavian; and all are built out of local marble. Although this

Fig. 3.2. Temple of Aphrodite, looking east toward Baba Dağı.

Fig. 3.3. Cult statue of Aphrodite.

ambitious program was probably a direct result of Aphrodisias's support of Rome in the Roman civil wars and of Zoilos's personal connections with Octavian, it was traditionally Hellenistic in overall conception. In other words, it represents the resumption of Hellenistic traditions made possible by the Roman Peace rather than a dramatic break with the Greek past.

In the wake of the establishment of the imperial system by Augustus and the successful succession of the next emperor, Tiberius, Aphrodisias emerged as a prosperous second-tier provincial city, able to compete with nearby towns such as Laodicea and Hierapolis to the east and Nysa and Stratoniceia to the west in emulation of older and more important administrative, commercial, and religious centers such as Ephesus and Pergamon. A second stage in the development of the city center shows the influence of new ideas of urban space and civic architecture characteristic of the Early and High Imperial periods (first and second centuries AD) in many parts of the Roman Empire. From the early first century AD onward, a number of new building projects were undertaken at Aphrodisias by a group of families whose names recur again and again in dedicatory and honorific inscriptions over the next several generations. These projects include the construction of

Fig. 3.4. South portico of Sebasteion after restoration, looking southwest.

Fig. 3.5. North Agora (green area in center), looking northwest.

the Sebasteion (the sanctuary of the imperial cult), a new public space along-side the Agora (the so-called South Agora), and a permanent stone auditorium for the Theater. The patrons of these buildings were presumably leading civic aristocrats, whose wealth must have resided primarily in local landhold-ings. As an imperial cult sanctuary, the Sebasteion clearly addresses the new reality of the world governed by Rome, and its architecture and sculpture were also strongly influenced by Roman models (fig. 3.4).[21] The enclosure of the Agora (today called the North Agora) was probably completed in the early first century AD, and thereafter this traditional Hellenistic public square remained essentially unchanged (fig. 3.5). The new stone auditorium

Fig. 3.6. Theater, looking southeast.

Fig. 3.7. Stadium, looking east.

of the Theater built in the first and early second century was supported by an elaborate series of rubble vaults, and a large public bath complex was built to the southeast, probably in the early to mid-second century (fig. 3.6). The Stadium was built on the northern edge of town in the mid- or late first century (fig. 3.7). It has a seating capacity of ca. 30,000 and is the best preserved of all ancient stadia. In structure and plan it is an experimental building largely supported in the traditional manner by earthen embankments rather than by vaulted structures, but with the unusual innovation of double-curved ends—a reminiscence, surely intentional, of the Roman amphitheater.[22]

The main focus of High Imperial building efforts in the city center was the large area between the North Agora and the Theater, which we call the

Fig. 3.8. South Agora with village of Geyre in background, looking northwest.

Fig. 3.9. Tetrapylon, looking north.

South Agora. By the early to mid-second century, this whole area had been enclosed by colonnaded porticoes and monumental buildings, surrounding a long pool (fig. 3.8). The area was dominated on the west by public baths of imperial type, dedicated to the emperor Hadrian, and on the east by a towering columnar façade, datable by its statuary decoration to the Antonine period. A civil basilica was built into the southwest corner of the area. The Temple of Aphrodite also received attention throughout the Early and High Imperial periods: completed as a traditional temple of the Ionic order in the early or mid-first century, in the Hadrianic period it was enclosed within a colonnaded court, dominated on its east side (like the South Agora) by a monumental, inward-facing, columnar façade. At a slightly later date, the enormous area east of the Temple was apparently walled off, with a large columnar entranceway, the so-called Tetrapylon, placed on the east side (fig. 3.9). Another substantial project was the construction in the Antonine and Severan periods of a new Bouleuterion (Council House) on the north side of the North Agora (fig. 3.10). This building may have replaced an earlier Bouleuterion on the same site, but its form, a semicircular covered theater, is of a new type, clearly influenced by the Roman form of the odeion.

Inscriptions from Aphrodisias provide valuable information about the social history of the city and its relations with the larger world. Of great importance is a series of documents carved on the north wall of the stage

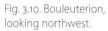

Fig. 3.10. Bouleuterion, looking northwest.

building of the Theater in the early to mid-third century AD. The earliest of these include copies of several letters of Octavian and of a senatorial decree bestowing special privileges on Aphrodisias, including tax-free status. Most of the other documents are copies of letters of later emperors confirming these privileges. By the early third century, thanks to a continuous local benefaction occasionally supplemented by imperial indulgence, as in the case of the baths dedicated to Hadrian, Aphrodisias had been transformed into a regional architectural showpiece, featuring a rich panoply of civic and religious buildings, sumptuously adorned with freestanding and relief sculpture, all carved largely out of local marble.

Territorial Boundaries and Roads

The definition of the territory of Aphrodisias was an important facet of the life of the city, especially given its tax-free status within the province of Asia. The only new information recorded by the survey project for the territorial boundaries of the city was the confirmation of a hypothesis, first proposed by L. and J. Robert, that in the second century AD the Aphrodisians built an aqueduct to tap the waters of the ancient Timeles River, located outside their own valley on the west edge of the neighboring plain of Tabae (discussed below). Although it is possible that Aphrodisias drew its water from the territory of a neighboring city, it seems more likely that the Timeles formed what would have been a logical boundary between Aphrodisias and the city of Herakleia Salbakes on the plain of Tabae, which features the river on its coins. The eastern boundary of our survey area may thus correspond at least in general terms with the eastern boundary of the territory of the city (see front flap). The other boundaries of the survey are also drawn along natural borders. The southwest plateau would presumably have belonged to Aphrodisias in the Roman period, if Bingeç is indeed correctly identified as Hellenistic Plarasa, and the southern edge of this plateau might have formed the border between Aphrodisias and the cities of the upper Harpasus River valley. To the west, the gorge that separates the upper from the lower Morsynus River valley could have marked the boundary with Antioch on the Maeander, and to the north, the Baba Dağı Ridge could have formed the boundary between Aphrodisias and the neighboring city of Attouda. The peak of Baba Dağı was marked by a Hellenistic sanctuary, and this, together with the orientation of the Temple of Aphrodite at Aphrodisias according to the mountain, suggests that Baba Dağı belonged to the territory of the city.

Evidence for the roads that connected Aphrodisias and its territory with neighboring cities and regions includes the Late Roman city gates, the topography of the urban cemeteries, the territorial fortifications, and the locations of rural settlements (see figs. 3.1, 1.11). Apparently the most important entranceway to Late Roman Aphrodisias was the West Gate, and it seems likely that the road that led out of this gate followed the path of an earlier Roman and perhaps even pre-Roman road. The distribution of tombs outside the city suggests that the road ran more or less due west, probably slightly south of the modern highway, until it approached the Morsynus River near the confluence of the Işıklar Çayı. From this point, it probably followed the path of the river until it reached Antioch on the Maeander, where it joined the main east-west highway connecting the Aegean coast with the Anatolian interior.

The Northeast Gate marks another entranceway to the city, and it may have been connected with two roads leading northward and northeastward toward the Baba Dağı Ridge, one toward the pass at Tekçam, the other toward Baba Dağı itself. A substantial necropolis extends approximately 2 km north of the city in the direction of modern Işıklar. This road may have continued along the same route as the modern road to Tekçam and the territory of Attouda. Another group of tombs lies to the northeast of Aphrodisias, along the road to the ancient (and modern) marble quarries just 2 km northeast of the city. This is the beginning of the most direct route from Aphrodisias to Baba Dağı, which runs from modern Palamutçuk to the citadel above Yeniköy, and then up a projecting spur to the Baba Dağı Ridge. Used today largely by shepherds, it must also have been known in antiquity.

The principal gate on the east side of Aphrodisias is known as the Southeast Gate, and it leads to another substantial necropolis, extending approximately 1 km to the southeast. This was presumably the beginning of the main road leading eastward to the plain of Tabae. The modern highway runs north of the Morsynus River (i.e., on the river's right bank), until it begins to climb toward the pass northwest of modern Yahşiler. The presence of the Late Classical or Hellenistic citadel east of modern Seki suggests that an ancient road also ran through this pass.

A modern road runs southward from Aphrodisias to the village of Ören. A number of tombs and other monuments have been observed along this road, but that may be misleading, since the areas farther afield on both sides of the road have not been explored. The locations of the watchtowers north and south of Ören do suggest, however, that this was also the route of an ancient road, which would have given access, among other things, to the substantial ancient and modern marble quarries west of Ören.

The last major gate in the walls of Aphrodisias is the Southwest Gate, and here too a line of tombs extending to the southwest for approximately 1 km probably marks the beginning of an ancient road. Possibly this road followed the same route as a modern road that crosses the river at one of the few places where it is easily forded. It may have been the major road leading south to the habitation sites and the marble and emery quarries near modern Çamarası—and beyond to Plarasa and the other communities of the southwest plateau.

Rural Settlement

The era of the emergence of towns in the region around Aphrodisias, in the second and first centuries BC, coincides with the earliest datable evidence for rural habitation besides tombs and territorial fortifications. In the course of our survey, we divided rural habitation sites into two broad categories, farmsteads and settlements, the former consisting only of concentrations of pottery sherds, tiles, and occasional architectural blocks with no visible in-situ architectural remains, the latter having the same characteristics as farmsteads but with the addition of visible in-situ remains, usually in the form of rubble walls. It should be noted that while the observable distinctions between what we called farmsteads and settlements are significant, they may have more to do with changing historical circumstances and different site-formation processes than with original size and function. In particular, the valley floor is more intensively cultivated today than the surrounding hills, with the result that originally very similar structures may be preserved very differently, with the lines of walls still traceable on hillside sites, while all that survives of valley sites are debris scatters. Thus many farmsteads and settlements may in fact originally have been sites of the same type—isolated rural farms or clusters of farms. The only larger ancient villages observed are those sites that exhibit a cluster of farmsteads or settlements in a single concentrated area, and, especially, those in which farmsteads and settlements are combined with other forms of evidence, particularly tombs. These include the sites at the modern villages of Bingeç (Plarasa) and Görle on the southwest plateau and a very pronounced cluster of points of interest on the south side of the Morsynus River valley, 3 km due south of Aphrodisias.

Systematic collection of surface finds was carried out at all settlements and at all farmsteads exhibiting evidence for large-scale agricultural processing, as well as at all sites intersected by the transects of the intensive survey. The general results of our survey of rural habitation sites are summed up in figures 3.11 and 3.12. Figure 3.11 is a map showing the locations of the 23 settlements identified on the survey; 20 of these were identified through the extensive survey, three through the intensive survey.

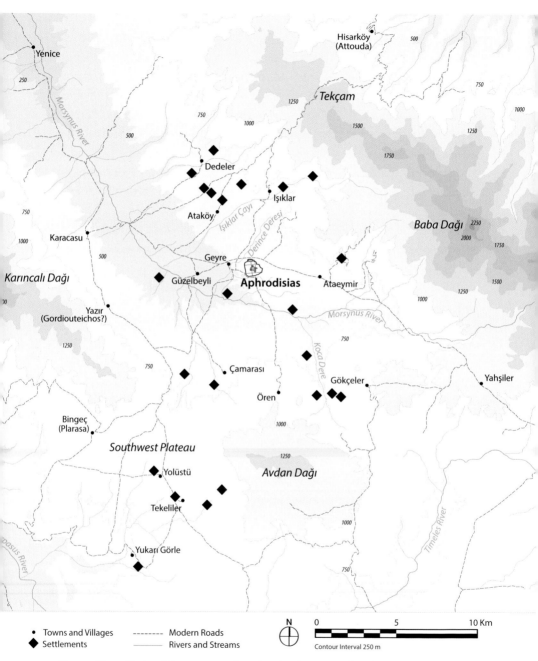

Fig. 3.11. Map of Aphrodisias survey region, showing locations of settlements.

They are concentrated on the hill-slopes overlooking the Morsynus River valley and on the plateau to the south, with only three settlements lying below 600 masl in elevation. Datable pottery was collected at 19 of the 23 settlements. Figure 3.12 is a map of the 33 farmsteads identified on the survey; we carried out systematic collection of pottery at 18 of these sites and were able to assign dates to these and five other farmstead sites.

Together with the territorial fortifications discussed in the previous chapter, this group of settlements and farmsteads comprises all the sites identified on the Aphrodisias Regional Survey where systematic collection of surface finds provided ceramic evidence for dating. With the notable exception of the prehistoric cave site, the Classical and Hellenistic tumuli, the territorial fortifications, and the post-antique (especially Ottoman) remains, most of the archaeological points of interest besides settlements and farmsteads recorded on the survey—tombs, isolated architectural blocks, isolated agricultural processing blocks, quarries, waterworks, and sanctuaries—can be dated to the Roman Imperial period.

What kind of picture does the evidence paint of the settlement history of the region? If we focus on the 42 datable settlements and farmsteads, we see that most of the sites in the hills to the north and south of Aphrodisias (16 out of 42) were occupied in the first century BC or earlier (11 out of 16 hillside sites, or 69 percent), and that in almost all of these (9 out of 11), the preponderance of the pottery dates to or before the Early Imperial period. Occupation on the valley floor tends to start later than occupation in the hills; only 6 out of 22 valley sites, or 27 percent, were definitely occupied before the Early Imperial period. On the other hand, most of these sites on the valley floor were occupied at least as late as the third or fourth centuries AD, and a number were occupied through Late Antiquity.

For the Hellenistic and Early Roman eras, then, regional settlement at Aphrodisias seems to conform to an understandable pattern. Concentrated in earlier periods in the more remote areas of the hills surrounding the valley and the plateau to the south, settlement moved down to the floor of the valley in Roman times, just as low-lying Aphrodisias came to overshadow highland Plarasa. Indeed, the farmsteads on the floor of the valley may

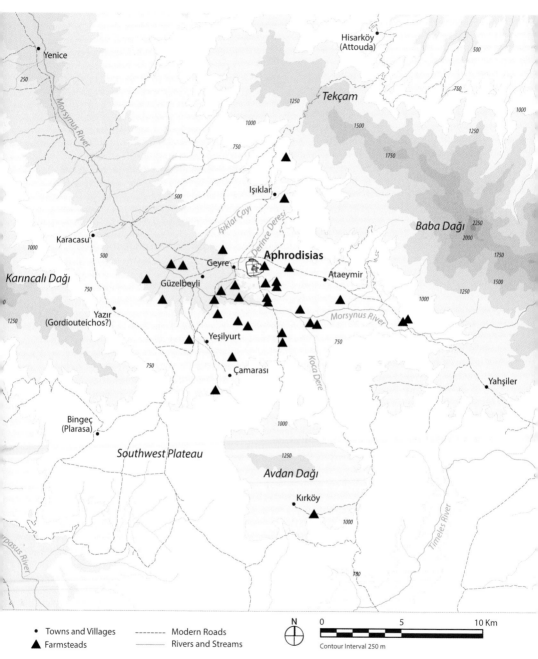

Fig. 3.12. Map of Aphrodisias survey region, showing locations of farmsteads.

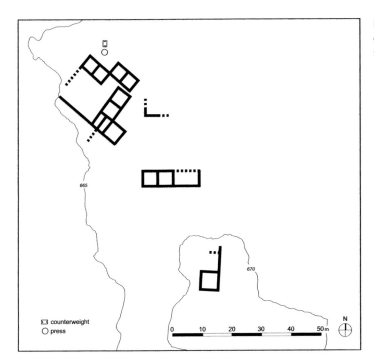

Fig. 3.13. Plan of Ataköy settlement.

have directly replaced the settlements in the surrounding hills, although the latter may also have remained seasonally inhabited. The growth of the city in the context of the Roman Peace provides one ready explanation for this apparent shift from habitation in the hills to habitation in the valley; the other is proximity to the region's most fertile agricultural soils, in an era in which the added security of a more remote habitation site was no longer a concern.

A good illustration of what rural occupation looked like in the hills to the north and south of Aphrodisias between the first century BC and the High Imperial period comes from a settlement located just 1 km north of the modern village of Ataköy (the settlement immediately north of Ataköy on fig. 3.11; fig. 3.13). It sits atop a low ridge, relatively close to Aphrodisias and easily accessible by gentle slopes on all but its western side. The ancient settlement has four surviving structures spread over an area approximately

Fig. 3.14. Crushing basin and counterweight block at Ataköy settlement.

110 m by 40 m. The largest structure, at the north end of the settlement, appears to have had at least nine rooms arranged along the sides of a roughly square court-yard. The walls were built of schist and are about 0.8 m thick. A crushing basin and counterweight block for the production of olive oil were found at the north edge of the site, probably originally inside a building (fig. 3.14; oil production is discussed in the section on agriculture below). The pottery from the Ataköy settlement indicates that occupation at the site was short-lived, since it all seems to belong to the first centuries BC and AD. Like the other rural settlements in the hills—as well as the territorial fortifications discussed in the previous chapter—the site was apparently abandoned at the time of the monumentalization of the city of Aphrodisias in the first century AD and never reoccupied.

What can be said about the density of rural settlement in the Hellenistic and Roman periods, and about the population of the valley as a whole? These kinds of questions are notoriously difficult to address, but a few speculative comments may be made. Estimates of the urban population of the city, based on the number of houses, the probable size of households, and the overall area of the city, range from about 6,500 to 12,500 persons. Any attempt to estimate the rural population of Aphrodisias is bound to be equally if not more speculative, especially since there was not always a distinction to be drawn between urban and rural residents. On the contrary, most of the inhabitants of the city certainly also possessed rural landholdings, and many may have lived on those rural landholdings for certain months of every year. That said, there must have been a significant number of people living in the territory of Aphrodisias who resided year-round on rural farms or in villages, traveling to Aphrodisias only on market or festival days, or for other special occasions. How large was this number? How were these rural residents distributed over the landscape? And how did the resulting pattern develop over time?

One inevitably problematic but still useful way to begin to address these questions is by analogy with modern population data for the region. In 2010, the population of the administrative district of Karacasu, whose borders are close to those of the survey region, was 20,389, with 6,108 people in the town of Karacasu itself (close to the lower estimates for the population of ancient Aphrodisias) and the rest distributed in villages throughout the countryside.[23] The results of our survey would suggest that the regional population was if anything more concentrated in a single urban center in antiquity than it is today. In the extensive survey, we found no site remotely approaching Aphrodisias in size, and it seems unlikely that any such ancient site lies beneath any of the modern villages; as already noted, no villages besides Bingeç and Görle had substantial ancient cemeteries associated with them or yielded significant numbers of inscriptions or other blocks. The results of the intensive survey are also consistent with the proposition that rural occupation of the area around Aphrodisias in the Roman period was no denser than modern occupation. Quite possibly it was considerably less dense. In Classical Greece, for example, ratios of urban to rural settlement of 1:1 are thought to have been the norm.[24] The urban and rural populations of the territory around Aphrodisias in the Roman period may also have been roughly equal, and if so, Aphrodisias would in this respect as in many others have remained true to well-established regional cultural patterns.

Agriculture (by Ian Lockey)

Rural settlement in the region around Aphrodisias concentrated naturally on exploitation of the region's most valuable natural resource: its arable land. The development of oleoculture, a major form of specialized agriculture, in the Hellenistic and Roman periods seems to have been limited to local market supply. Only in Late Antiquity, with the appearance

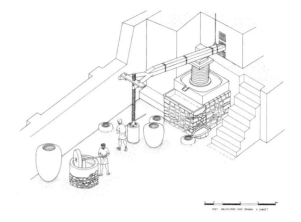

of one or more large olive oil factories on the southwest plateau, did
the region apparently begin to produce olive oil for export, in this case
probably for the new imperial capital at Constantinople (discussed in the
next chapter).

The area around Aphrodisias is climatically well suited to olive cultivation because of its hot summers, cold but not freezing winters, and
annual precipitation of approximately 0.45 m. In addition, the iron-rich
soil of some parts of the Morsynus River valley is ideal for olive growth.
Today, approximately 3,200 ha are assigned to oleoculture in the modern territory of Karacasu. Modern production levels indicate olive oil's
importance to the economy of the region: 800,000 trees produce an
annual yield of approximately 20,000 tons of olives.[25] These numbers
do not of course necessarily correspond with ancient production levels,
but the evidence collected by the survey shows that olive oil production
has been an important activity in the valley since at least the Hellenistic period. A handful of inscriptions from Aphrodisias attest the use of
olive oil for purposes typical of a Graeco-Roman city: the liquid was
given as a prize for competitive events, distributed for free in gymnasia,
and offered in celebration of the completion of building projects, such
as the Timeles aqueduct.[26] The excavations at Aphrodisias have revealed
olive oil presses of Early or Middle Byzantine date (fig. 3.15), but only

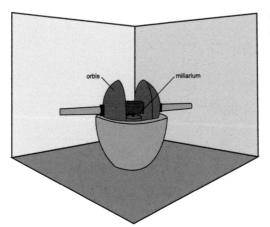

Fig. 3.16. Reconstruction of *trapetum* system from Pompeii.

the results of the survey provide direct evidence for oil production in Hellenistic and Roman times and offer a fuller picture of valley-wide production and use in all periods.

The technology of olive oil production remained fairly constant from antiquity until the nineteenth century, making it difficult to date olive oil processing equipment with certainty. Fortunately, surface pottery associated with in-situ press facilities does provide broad dating evidence in a number of cases. The typical method for olive oil production in the Morsynus River valley, as indicated by the large number of counterweight blocks discovered on the regional survey, involved the lever press, explained below.

Once the olives had been harvested in early winter, they were stored prior to processing and allowed to ripen. When ready for processing, the olives were transferred to a crushing basin. This was a large stone vessel roughly worked on the outside, with a shallow interior basin lined with grooves (see fig. 3.14). As noted by the Roman author Cato, if olives were crushed together with their pits in the basin, the taste of the oil became bitter.[27] To avoid this problem, the system known as the *trapetum* was invented, whereby grooves were carved into the side and bottom of the crushing basin to collect the pits while the grinding stones removed the flesh (fig. 3.16). Each basin had a pair of hemispherical grinding stones (*orbes*) made specifically for it. They were

Fig. 3.17. Tear-drop-shaped press bed found near modern settlement of Ataeymir.

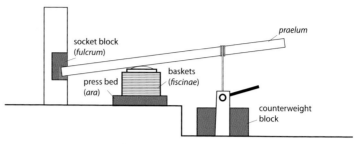

Fig. 3.18. Reconstruction of a lever-press system.

socket block
(*fulcrum*)

praelum

press bed
(*ara*)

baskets
(*fiscinae*)

counterweight
block

Fig. 3.19. Socket block at Koca Ören settlement.

Fig. 3.20. Counterweight block at Çatak Tepesi settlement.

held on a wooden crossbeam, which revolved on a central post-with-socket (*miliarium*) in the center of the basin.

The crushed olive pulp was then removed from the basin and loaded into woven nets or flat baskets (*fiscinae*) and piled up onto the press bed (*ara*) (fig. 3.17). A heavy wooden beam (*praelum*) was winched down to press on the olive pulp held in the nets, and the oil ran into the channels of the press bed and out of the spout into a settling tank (fig. 3.18). The socket block (*fulcrum*) was built into the back wall of the press room (fig. 3.19) and constitutes the visible remains of the anchor for the wooden press beam. At the other end, the beam was attached to the counterweight block by a windlass made of wood and rope; two tapering wooden posts fixed the windlass to the counterweight block (fig. 3.20). As the windlass was tightened, it exerted increasing pressure on the olive pulp to extract as much oil as possible. Water was a key component of the final phases of the production process, both for separating the olive oil from the bitter dregs (*amurca*) in the settling tank—the oil floated on top of the water, and the dregs sank to the bottom—and for cleaning the nets or baskets. Large cisterns are found at two settlements, Koca Ören (1.4 km east of the village of Tekeliler on the southwest plateau; see fig. 3.11) and Kadıkerim Mevkii (2.5 km west of the village of Güzelbeyli in the Morsynus River valley; see fig. 3.11), and other sites are located near natural water sources, such as the village of Yıkıntı Tepesi (2.2 km east of the village of Ören on the southeast side of the Morsynus River valley; see fig. 3.11), situated just above the Koca Dere.

In total, 90 separate points of interest associated with agricultural processing (olive oil or wine production) were located on the regional survey (fig. 3.21). These range from parts of presses divorced from their original contexts (the bulk of the evidence) to in-situ press facilities. Thirty-three, or just over one-third of the total number of sites, were identified in the intensive survey of the area within a one-kilometer radius of the center of the city of Aphrodisias (omitting the city itself). The sites that exhibited evidence for agricultural processing fall into four categories: isolated stone press and mill elements, farmsteads, settlements, and possible monasteries. It is important to note, however, that sites with evidence for agricultural processing make up

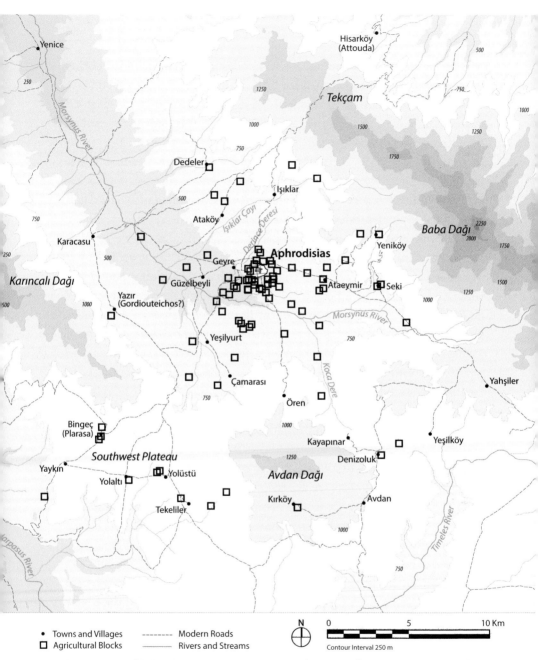

Fig. 3.21. Map of Aphrodisias survey region, showing locations of remains associated with agricultural processing.

only about half the total number of rural habitation sites identified during the survey. Only 13 out of 25 settlements, 17 out of 33 farmsteads, and 2 of the 10 churches and possible monasteries exhibit evidence of this kind. Of course, not every rural farm had its own wine or olive press. These rather expensive facilities may have been associated principally with larger farms or estates, with villages where they would have served the needs of whole communities of farmers, or (in Late Antiquity) with monasteries.

In addition, some of the equipment identified by the survey could also have been used to produce other commodities, particularly wine. Wine and olive oil presses used similar sets of equipment, and some scholars question whether it is even possible to tell the difference between them.[28] The presence of a crushing basin may indicate that a set of press equipment was more likely to have been used specifically for olive oil production.[29] Twenty-two crushing basins were found in the region around Aphrodisias, but the bulk of the evidence consists of counterweight blocks and of press elements containing sockets for press beams.

The principal types of sites with evidence for agricultural processing are settlements and farmsteads. As noted above, the majority of the settlements in the Morsynus River valley are found in the hills to the north and south of Aphrodisias and date to the later Hellenistic and Early Roman periods. The settlement near Ataköy discussed above, which contained a crushing basin and counterweight block, is a typical example (see figs. 3.13–14). By contrast, most farmsteads occupy the valley floor and date to the Roman Imperial period. The southwest plateau exhibits a slightly different settlement pattern. In addition to settlements, two new and specialized site types can be found there: the olive oil "factory" and the fortified farm. These appear only in the Late Antique period, and they seem to point to an intensification of olive oil production at this time, perhaps in response to the growing state and commercial markets at Constantinople. These new settlement types will be treated in more detail in the next chapter.

The different types of rural habitation identified by the survey—settlements, farmsteads, olive oil "factories," fortified farms, and monasteries—therefore seem to correspond to different periods of occupation. The movement from settlements in the hills to farmsteads on the valley floor corresponds with the establishment and growth of Aphrodisias itself. In addition to its effects on agriculture and rural settlement, the impact of the development of Aphrodisias on the surrounding countryside is most clearly seen in the exploitation of two other valuable local resources: building stone and water.

Marble (by Leah Long)

The area around Aphrodisias is remarkably rich in marble, which is still quarried to this day. Indeed, since modern quarrying operations are often located on or near ancient quarry sites, the ongoing exploitation of regional marble beds gives the investigation of ancient quarries special urgency.

Sources of high-quality marble lie just 2 km from the city (the so-called City Quarries), and by the Late Hellenistic period a local tradition of marble sculpture had already taken root. Large-scale quarrying began in earnest in the later first century BC, with the construction of the Temple of Aphrodite and a number of other buildings associated with the patronage of C. Julius Zoilos. Sculptures signed by Aphrodisian carvers have been found as far away as Rome and the emperor Hadrian's villa at Tivoli, but local sculptors were also busy at home, and the excavations have revealed hundreds of monuments of great variety and virtuosity, including statues of gods, heroes, emperors, orators, philosophers, and boxers, as well as a broad range of ornamental and figured reliefs. Even after the mid-third century, when the development of Aphrodisias began to slow considerably, freshly quarried stone continued to be used for select sculptures and architectural elements up to the late fifth or early sixth century AD.

The so-called City Quarries, 2 km north of Aphrodisias, have long been known and are the subject of ongoing study. The regional survey revealed that Aphrodisias drew on eight additional local marble quarries scattered throughout the upper Morsynus River valley (fig. 3.22). It has sometimes been suggested that marble from Aphrodisias was sold on the export market, and that profit from this enterprise was one source of the

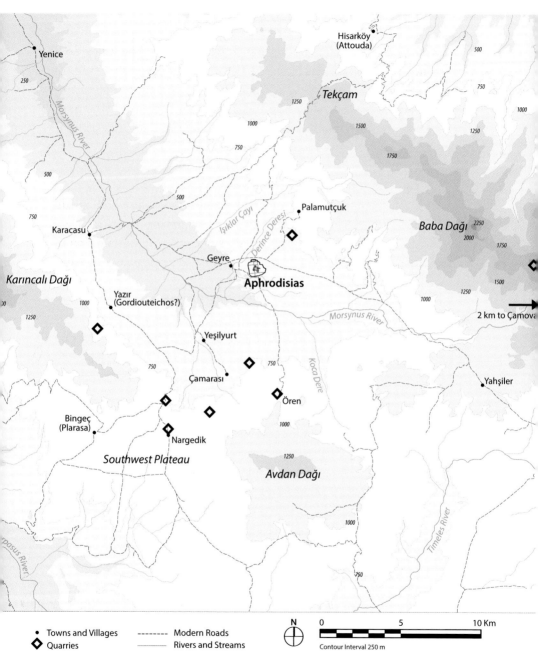

Fig. 3.22. Map of Aphrodisias survey region, showing locations of quarries.

Fig. 3.23. City Quarries north of Aphrodisias, looking south-east.

city's prosperity in Roman times. But even though we now know that the marble resources exploited in antiquity were more widespread than previously recognized, careful study of all the known ancient quarries suggests that they were still only adequate to meet local needs. While Aphrodisias apparently did export marble for sculpture to marble-poor cities elsewhere in southwestern Asia Minor, such as Sagalassos, and perhaps on occasion for the use of Aphrodisian sculptors working farther afield, Aphrodisias is unlikely ever to have been a major marble exporter. Like the produce of its farmland, Aphrodisian marble was largely intended for local use. In fact, local resources were so abundant and varied that expensive marbles widely available on the open market were never imported into Aphrodisias for architectural decoration, though they were in other cities across the region.

The City Quarries are the largest of the known ancient quarries in the region, and their proximity to the city, together with the local topography, rendered large-scale exploitation of marble in the public architecture of Aphrodisias unusually inexpensive (figs. 3.22–23). The quarries lie just 2 km north of the city, and the steady but gentle slope that connects them is ideal for transport. This series of seven individual quarries covers an area of about 1 km^2 and is clustered in groups on three adjacent hills at eleva-

Fig. 3.24. Worked face of quarry near Hançam.

tions of around 700 masl. We estimate that approximately 55,000 m³ of medium-grained white and grayish white and fine-grained blue-gray marbles were extracted from the City Quarries in antiquity. Pickmarked quarry faces more than 20 m high are visible in places, and spoil heaps line the perimeters of the largest quarries. The Christian crosses and prayers inscribed on one quarry face, presumably by quarry workers, suggest that the City Quarries remained an active site of industry well into Late Antiquity.

Five of the newly discovered quarries are situated in the hills on the south side of Morsynus River valley at elevations between 745 and 961 masl, in an uncultivable zone that may have been largely uninhabited in antiquity, as it is today. They are located at distances of 5 to 11 km from Aphrodisias as the crow flies. Together these quarries yielded approximately 55,000 m³ of marble, equal to the amount extracted from the City Quarries. Traces of ancient quarrying techniques are clearly visible in many of these quarries, such as the worked faces at the quarries near Hançam, where a thick marble deposit was followed below ground level to extract a series of blocks (figs. 3.22, 3.24).

The most dramatically sited quarries are located at the edge of the survey and watershed boundary, on the slopes of Baba Dağı at an elevation of 2,007 masl and a distance of 17 km from Aphrodisias (figs. 3.22,

Fig. 3.25. View of Baba Dağı quarries, looking southwest over Morsynus River valley.

Fig. 3.26. Abandoned column fragments in breccia marble at Baba Dağı quarries.

3.25). Approximately 750 m³ of medium- to coarse-grained, blue-gray and white marble, ranging from mottled to breccia, were removed from the Baba Dağı quarries, some in blocks more than 3 m long (fig. 3.26). Another group of quarries is situated on the eastern side of Baba Dağı at a place called Çamova Tepe, at an elevation of 1,472 masl and a distance of 22 km as the crow flies from Aphrodisias. These quarries yielded approximately 3,000 m³ of medium-grained purplish gray and white breccia marble. This stone is virtually indistinguishable visually from the highly prized purple and white *pavonazzetto* extracted from the famous quarries at Dokimeion in central Phrygia, which were owned by the Roman state and operated by imperial bureaucrats and the army.

Most of the marble quarried in the region belongs to a single geological formation—the Mesozoic Milas Formation. Only one quarry identified

Fig. 3.27. Yazır quarry, looking southeast.

in our survey, near the modern village of Yazır, belongs to the underlying Paleozoic Göktepe Formation (figs. 3.22, 3.27). The Yazır quarry is located on a steep hill below a Late Classical citadel, described in the previous chapter, at an elevation of 919 masl and a distance of 11 km from Aphrodisias. Approximately 6,750 m^3 of medium- to coarse-grained white and fine- to medium-grained mottled blue-gray marble were extracted here. Like the marbles from Çamova Tepe, those from the Yazır quarry resemble celebrated colored marbles from Dokimeion, in this case the blue and white *kaplan postu*, which was exported to the Roman cities of central and southern Asia Minor. Transportation to Aphrodisias from the City Quarries or the quarries on the south side of the valley would not have posed great logistical problems, but the topography of the quarries at Yazır, in the west, and at Baba Dağı and Çamova Tepe, in the east, presented serious challenges. At Yazır, marble scree was thrown down a steep hillside to facilitate transportation, and slipways are still visible above a mountain stream below, which is littered with broken blocks. Transportation from these more distant and topographically isolated quarries would have incurred greater costs than from the white marble sources closer to the city, but the colored marbles from these quarries would still have been significantly less expensive than imported stone carried up the Maeander valley from the coast. Despite the value of the colored marbles, these quarries are too small to have ever been exploited for more than a local or regional market.

The marbles of the Aphrodisias region have two very distinct isotopic signatures, which correspond to the two marble-bearing units of the survey region, the Mesozoic Milas Formation and the Paleozoic Göktepe Formation. The isotopic signatures of samples taken from the quarries were compared to those of archaeological samples taken from monuments inside the city of Aphrodisias to determine whether the stone from buildings and statues with secure dates and archaeological contexts could be traced to individual quarries.[30] The monuments of Aphrodisias are composed primarily of white marble, along with local blue-gray marble, limestone, quartz, and schist. The white marble seems to have come largely from the local quarries, and most quarry products appear to have been reserved for local building projects and statue monuments. Fine-grained blue-gray marbles were also used for architectural elements and special commissions, such as a famous statue of a horse, apparently carved out of stone from the City Quarries.[31] While most of the local quarries consciously targeted white marbles, those at Yazır, Baba Dağı, and Çamova Tepe offered marbles with unique color properties. The archaeological samples taken from mottled blue-gray architectural blocks all fall within the same unique range of isotopic values as the samples from the quarry at Yazır (fig. 3.28). It therefore seems certain that the Yazır quarry was the primary source of the mottled blue and white marble widely used at Aphrodisias from the early second through the third century. Marbles from both Yazır and Çamova Tepe resembled the internationally famous colored marbles from the imperial quarries at Dokimeion and made it possible for local builders

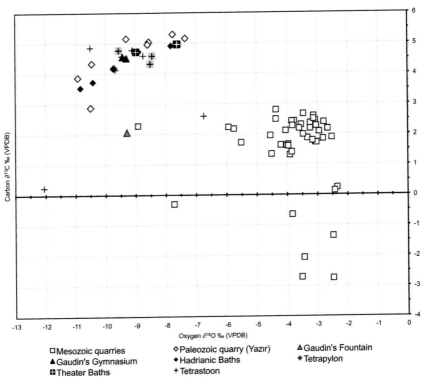

Fig 3.28. Chart (cross plot) showing isotopic signatures of samples from mottled blue-gray marble architectural elements at Aphrodisias compared with samples from quarry at Yazır.

to achieve with local stone the same effect that other cities could only attain by importing materials at great expense.

Water Supply and Aqueducts
(by Angela Commito and Felipe Rojas)

Another benefit of the location of the city—and presumably one if its raisons d'être from the prehistoric era onward—is its local water supply, including both the high water table and the seasonal streams that run nearby, particularly the Morsynus River itself. For two and a half centuries after the founding of the city, water from wells, cisterns, springs, and streams met the needs of the residents of Aphrodisias and of people living

throughout the valley. By the late first century AD, however, the growing city required a more abundant and reliable water supply. This demand
could be satisfied only with the construction of aqueducts that tapped
sources located farther and farther away, eventually extending as far as the
neighboring plain of Tabae to the southeast (fig. 3.29). At least three aqueducts were built in the Roman period to conduct water over long distances
primarily to supply the residents of Aphrodisias. Two additional aqueducts
may have each supplied a village, farmstead, or villa during the Roman,
Late Antique, or Medieval period. The sixth and final aqueduct identified
by the survey seems to have fed two small baths at Aphrodisias in the
Ottoman period and is discussed in chapter 6.

The two earliest aqueducts are named after the modern villages where
their remains have been found: Seki and Işıklar. They were likely constructed in the first century AD, in association with one or more bath complexes and an urban water-flow management system (including gutters,
canals, and reservoirs or holding ponds) known from inscriptions found
at Aphrodisias, as well as from archaeological evidence.[32] Both aqueducts
appear to have run in non-pressurized open conduits and are located at
elevations adequate to supply the city. The Seki aqueduct was at least 9
km long and probably tapped the abundant groundwater-fed springs to
the east of Aphrodisias that are still a main source of water for agriculture
and household consumption in the valley today. The extant remains of the
Seki aqueduct include a bridge located 8.5 km east of Aphrodisias (1.5 km
southeast of the village of Seki), just north of the main road through the
valley (figs. 3.29–31). The bridge crosses a tributary of the Morsynus River
and sits at an elevation of 705 masl, more than 280 m higher than Aphrodisias. Constructed of mortared rubble faced with petit appareil masonry
(consisting of small squared blocks set in mortar), the bridge is 6 m high
and extends 15 m across the streambed below. The structure is well preserved because it was incorporated into a road bridge during the Ottoman
period, when a second arched bridge was built flush against its northeast
side. The composite structure was given a pitched profile and resurfaced for
use by foot and wheeled traffic.

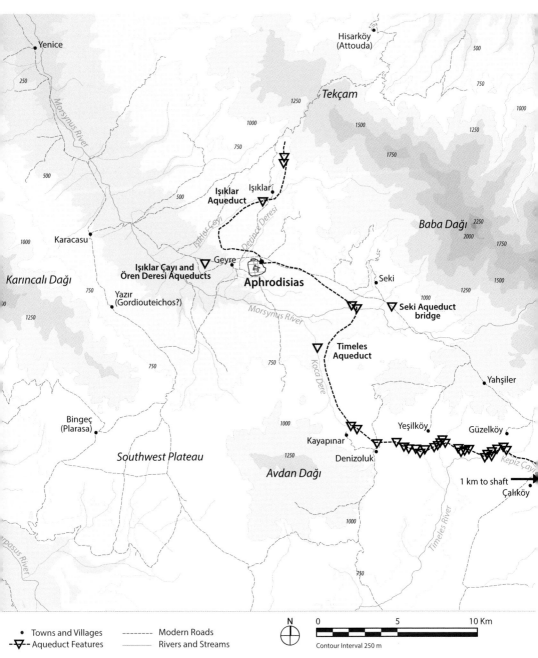

Fig. 3.29. Map of Aphrodisias survey region, showing locations of aqueducts.

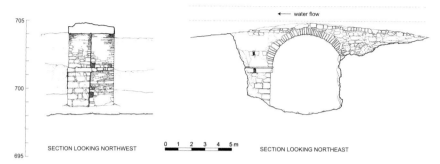

SECTION LOOKING NORTHWEST

← water flow

0 1 2 3 4 5 m

SECTION LOOKING NORTHEAST

Fig. 3.30. Section drawings of preserved bridge of Seki aqueduct.

Fig. 3.31. Seki aqueduct bridge, looking north.

Fig. 3.32. Standing pier of Işıklar aqueduct bridge, looking south-west.

The Işıklar aqueduct collected water from the hills on the north side of the valley at the base of Baba Dağı, which is snowcapped as late as June every year, and carried it to Aphrodisias along a route at least 10 km in length. The extant remains of the Işıklar aqueduct include a tunnel carved through bedrock and the pier of an aqueduct bridge built of mortared rubble set in courses and faced with petit appareil masonry (figs. 3.29, 3.32). The bridge would have originally been more than 42 m long and 15 m high. Once these structures had been identified by the survey, the likely route of the aqueduct was reconstructed using predictive modeling based on least-cost analysis (see fig. 3.29). The survey then identified what appears to be the remains of another bridge of this aqueduct, located almost exactly on the predicted route and therefore verifying the model.

The most substantial and well-preserved aqueduct carried water to Aphrodisias from a river called the Yenidere Çayı in the neighboring plain of Tabae to the southeast. This must be the aqueduct commemorated by coins and inscriptions from the city documenting plans for the construction of an aqueduct in AD 124 and 125 and the "introduction" of the Timeles River into Aphrodisias in the AD 160s or slightly later.[33] It therefore seems certain, as L. and J. Robert conjectured half a century ago,[34] that the Timeles River should be identified with the modern Yenidere Çayı in the plain of Tabae, and that this aqueduct tunneled through the chain of hills separating the plain of Tabae from the Morsynus River valley to bring the waters of the Timeles River to Aphrodisias. Along the way, the so-called Timeles aqueduct traveled more than 25 km through tunnels up to 2 km long and 50 m deep and across at least a dozen bridges up to 27 m high.

Once we had identified some of the remains of the Timeles aqueduct, we used predictive modeling to reconstruct its likely route from the source to the city (see fig. 3.29). The source is probably located somewhere in the vicinity of a modern dam built at the point where a tributary stream called the Kepiz Çayı joins the Timeles River, not far from the village of Güzelköy. According to local residents, until quite recently this tributary stream and its headwaters fed canals that powered a series of Ottoman mills located in the area. Alternatively, the source could be located farther east, around

Fig. 3.33.
Subterranean
masonry con-
duit of Timeles
aqueduct visi-
ble along road
cut near Kepiz
Çayı, looking
northeast.

the village of Çalıköy, where the survey documented a masonry-lined shaft connected to a rock-cut tunnel, or about 5 km farther east, at a well-watered place known as Kırkpınar, or "Forty Springs," an important source of water for residents of the Tavas plain today.

The construction of a modern road along the north bank of the Kepiz Çayı, following the same path as the aqueduct, has revealed sections of its originally subterranean masonry conduit, as well as two horizontal access tunnels used during the construction of the aqueduct and possibly also for maintenance (fig. 3.33). After following the north bank of the Kepiz Çayı, the aqueduct turned to the northwest and entered a tunnel that ran up to 50 m underground for almost 2 km through a wide, flat plateau south of the village of Yahşiler. Over this distance, on top of the plateau, mounds of rock chips at ground level mark the course of the aqueduct deep below the surface. Three of these mounds, each about 10 m in diameter and at least 2 m tall, are highly visible features in the landscape and can be seen even in satellite imagery (fig. 3.34). These mounds are heaps of backdirt (or spoil) created as construction crews dug deep shafts from the surface down to the level of the aqueduct tunnel. Creating vertical shafts rather than

Fig. 3.34. Satellite image showing three mounds of rock chips (right) and masonry-lined shaft (second from left), marking route of Timeles aqueduct tunnel, together with remains of bridge (far left) where aqueduct emerged from tunnel to cross a narrow valley (© 2010 Google, © 2011 DigitalGlobe).

boring straight through the plateau opened up multiple work surfaces to facilitate surveying the orientation and gradient of the tunnel, expedite the tunneling process, and provide air to the workers and exits for the removal of backdirt. Though only five shafts have been securely identified, as many as 19 shafts, spaced at intervals of 90–100 m, may have been created in the process of digging this tunnel.

After emerging from the tunnel to cross two bridges over a narrow valley, the aqueduct returned underground for another 1 km until it once again appeared on a series of four bridges spanning deep gorges near the village of Yeşilköy. Like all the Roman-period aqueduct bridges in the region, these are constructed of mortared rubble set in courses and faced with petit appareil masonry. The aqueduct first crossed a poorly preserved bridge that was originally composed of two tiers, with a lower arch supporting perhaps four arches above, topped by the conduit. Traces of the conduit indicate that the bridge was about 65 m long and 27 m high,

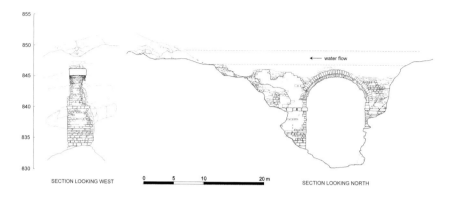

Fig. 3.35. Section drawings of best-preserved bridge of Timeles aqueduct, near Yeşilköy.

making it the longest and tallest bridge recorded by the survey, comparable in height to the famous aqueduct bridge of Segovia, which is 28.5 m
high. After returning underground for 190 m, the aqueduct then passed
over the best-preserved bridge, with an arch that remains intact and can
still be crossed on foot (figs. 3.35–36). This bridge is 36 m long and almost
17 m high above the gorge below. In this area the underground tunnel
and masonry conduit of the aqueduct are preserved for almost 150 m (fig.
3.37). The builders first excavated a tunnel through the bedrock and then
built the masonry conduit inside, topped by a barrel vault constructed
over a wooden frame. Here, as elsewhere along the aqueduct, the conduit
is 1.4 m wide and at least 1.9 m high and is built of rectangular blocks cut
from the local bedrock. About 1.5 km farther along the aqueduct, the conduit crossed a bridge near the village of Denizoluk (fig. 3.38). Originally
more than 50 m long, the bridge carried the conduit an estimated 18 m
above the streambed below and is supported by a masonry buttress on its
south side, likely a later addition. After crossing this bridge, the aqueduct
returned underground, where its route is indicated by a series of shafts
visible on the surface. One of these shafts is cut through the bedrock and
must have originally extended down about 50 m to the aqueduct conduit
running below (fig. 3.39). Now filled in with eroded soil, the shaft can still
be entered to a depth of about 13 m.

Fig. 3.36. Best-preserved bridge of Timeles aqueduct, near Yeşilköy, looking southwest.

Fig. 3.38. Bridge of the Timeles aqueduct near Denizoluk, looking northeast.

Fig. 3.37. Masonry conduit of Timeles aqueduct inside tunnel near Yeşilköy, looking northeast.

Fig. 3.39. Rock-cut shaft of Timeles aqueduct, near Denizoluk.

The bridges, tunnels, and shafts discussed so far are all located on the edge of the plain of Tabae, to the southeast of and outside the Morsynus River valley. The next structures identified by the survey are located inside the Morsynus River valley, near the village of Kayapınar. These remains include the backdirt pile of a shaft and a section of tunnel, visible at the beginning of a large streambed known as the Koca Dere. The aqueduct therefore must have traveled underground from the plain of Tabae into the Morsynus River valley by piercing a relatively low saddle in the series of hills that forms the boundary between these two valleys, near the village of Denizoluk. Two additional aqueduct bridges were recorded inside the Morsynus River valley, located on streams that feed into the Morsynus River from the northeast. No further remains of the aqueduct have been identified between these bridges and the city.

Our initial estimate for the potential discharge of the Timeles aqueduct is 157,000 m^3 of water each day, only about 30,000 m^3 less per day than the Aqua Claudia or Aqua Anio Novus in Rome; revised calculations suggest the discharge may have been considerably less, at somewhere between 60,000 and 90,000 m^3 per day.[35] In either case, this was a voluminous aqueduct, which, along with the Seki and Işıklar aqueducts that also served the city, was probably built to bring the majority of its waters to the estimated 6,500 to 12,500 residents of Aphrodisias itself. Among other functions, these aqueducts supplied bath complexes within the city, such as the Hadrianic Baths, as well as fountains and an enormous pool that ran down the South Agora.

However, there is some evidence that the Timeles aqueduct may have been tapped along its route, if not to irrigate crops, then perhaps to supply rural settlements or small-scale industrial activities located along its path, possibly after the aqueduct no longer supplied Aphrodisias. This evidence includes a small bridge encased in calcareous deposits, which could indicate that the aqueduct was tapped at this point, and a subterranean masonry conduit located along the west bank of the Koca Dere. The latter is situated very close to, but not directly on, the likely route of the Timeles aqueduct as suggested by our predictive model. This conduit could be a branch of the Timeles aqueduct, built to supply a nearby settlement, or

Fig. 3.40. Masonry conduit of Ören Deresi aqueduct, looking northwest.

it could be a reconfiguration of the aqueduct constructed in Late Antiquity or the Medieval period. Furthermore, at least two additional aqueducts were built in the valley to serve people living in the countryside. The remains of two subterranean mortared rubble masonry conduits, named the Işıklar Çayı and Ören Deresi aqueducts, are located at elevations that are too low to have served Aphrodisias at all (see fig. 3.29). The conduit of the Ören Deresi aqueduct, exposed along a streambed, even includes the remains of a vertical inspection shaft (fig. 3.40). These two aqueducts must have provided water to one or more of the nearby Roman, Late Antique, or Medieval settlements, villas, or farmsteads identified by the survey.

Like olive oil and marble, water was an important natural resource that was extracted locally and consumed locally, and therefore serves as a useful template for thinking about how most natural resources were exploited by ancient towns the size of Aphrodisias—that is, with populations of between 6,500 and 12,500 people—during the Late Hellenistic and Roman periods. Though the production and consumption of all three of these resources seems to have served only the people living within the region, they were nonetheless extracted and used at levels far above mere subsistence needs. Olive oil and water symbolized the wealth of the land, which was in turn the source of the prosperity that made it possible to sustain the labor force responsible for the widespread use of marble at

Aphrodisias. Providing the city with a copious water supply was not only a municipal duty but also a means by which wealthy Aphrodisians could promote themselves as public philanthropists. Like olive oil and marble, water also entered the city in volumes that far exceeded the subsistence requirements of its inhabitants. Produced and consumed in excess of basic needs, these local natural resources provided the basic building blocks for a certain Graeco-Roman urban lifestyle that spread across Asia Minor beginning in the Late Hellenistic period.

Cemeteries
(by Peter De Staebler, Christopher Ratté, and Heather Turnbow)

The earliest evidence for the development of cemeteries in the immediate environs of Aphrodisias takes the form of stray finds of anthemion stelai (floral gravestones), statues of lions, and funerary inscriptions of the sixth and subsequent centuries BC. It is not until after the founding of the city, however, that actual tomb structures are found in situ. Only two such tombs are datable by inscriptions. One, located just outside the west City Wall, is a platform probably for a sarcophagus identified by the accompanying inscription as the monument of Julius Aurelius Charidemos Julianus, datable by the letter forms and nomenclature to the second or third century AD.[36] The other, a subterranean barrel vault in a cemetery northeast of the city, is the tomb of the fifth-century Christian bishop Theopropius (see next chapter).[37] Most of the remaining in-situ tombs are datable only on general architectural grounds to the Late Hellenistic and Roman periods.

The suburban cemeteries of Aphrodisias lined the major roads radiating out of the city for distances of 2 km or more beyond the City Wall. They are attested both by in-situ tombs (approximately 75) and by whole or, in the vast majority of cases, fragmentary sarcophagi (approximately 150) (figs. 3.41–42). The majority of the tombs are barrel-vaulted hypogea (underground tomb chambers) of a type familiar from other regional sites, such as Magnesia on the Maeander and Ephesus. These hypogea are generally built of small mortared blocks of marble or schist, and they range in width from 1.88 m to 4.95 m, though most are 2–3 m wide. A small number of

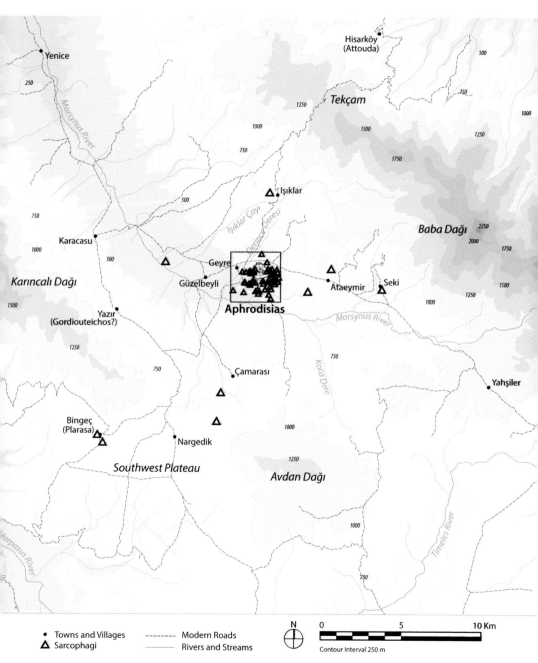

Fig. 3.41. Map of Aphrodisias survey region, showing findspots of sarcophagi.

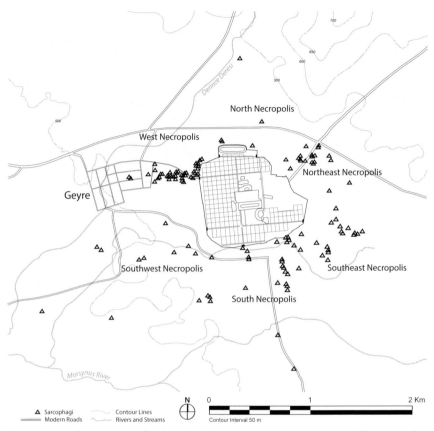

Fig. 3.42. Map of necropoleis of Aphrodisias, showing locations of tombs and findspots of sarcophagi.

tombs have more complex arrangements of multiple chambers, and in a few cases, pier foundations visible in the corners of the hypogea give evidence for monumental superstructures. None of these superstructures survives in situ, however, in large part because the cemeteries of Aphrodisias were systematically quarried for building materials in the mid-fourth century AD for the City Wall.[38] Nevertheless, the blocks reused in the walls attest a rich variety of conventional funerary monuments, ranging from simple sarcophagus platforms to more elaborate columnar monuments, such as the "temple tombs" of nearby Hierapolis and many other sites in Asia Minor.

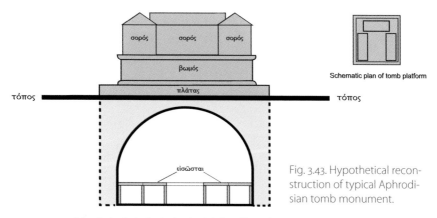

Fig. 3.43. Hypothetical reconstruction of typical Aphrodisian tomb monument.

In addition to in-situ monuments and displaced architectural blocks, inscriptions on sarcophagi provide another source of information for local tomb architecture. Many of these inscriptions begin by mentioning architectural elements such as a platform, a raised pedestal, burial niches or *loculi*, or a "place" on which the tomb stands. Other types of blocks from funerary monuments also contain informative inscriptions, many of which include references to the placement of the sarcophagus itself. These inscriptions, together with the evidence of more fully preserved monuments from other sites in Asia Minor, make it possible to envision the appearance of a hypothetical Aphrodisian tomb monument composed of the following major elements (fig. 3.43):

- σορός (*soros*), the sarcophagus.
- τόπος (*topos*), "place." Refers in general to the plot of land on which a monument is built.
- πλάτας (*platas*), a platform. Usually described as supporting a sarcophagus or other structure.
- βωμός (*bōmos*), "altar." At Aphrodisias and Hierapolis, refers to a built structure supporting a sarcophagus.
- εἰσώστη (*eisōstē*), a burial space or *loculus*, a term found only at Aphrodisias. Usually located beneath the sarcophagus, either within or underneath the *platas* or *bōmos*.

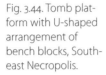

Fig. 3.44. Tomb platform with U-shaped arrangement of bench blocks, Southeast Necropolis.

While sarcophagi in Roman Italy and mainland Greece were commonly placed inside chamber tombs, sarcophagi in Roman Asia Minor were often displayed in the open air, on top of platforms, pedestals, or other supporting structures, in a practice that seems to originate with the Lycian sarcophagus monuments of the fifth and fourth centuries BC. In the second century AD, with the large-scale production and use of sarcophagi across the Roman world, inhabitants of many parts of Asia Minor retained the concept of raised sarcophagi while also adopting selected elements of Roman tomb design, including the placement of sarcophagi inside built chamber tombs. At Aphrodisias, however, both archaeological and epigraphic evidence indicates primarily aboveground display of sarcophagi. Numerous funerary sites in the necropoleis of Aphrodisias consist of sarcophagus fragments found in association with architectural elements such as columns, bench blocks, and large marble slabs, often above or in proximity to a built underground tomb chamber. Funerary inscriptions generally place the *soros* (sarcophagus) on top of a *platas* (platform) or *bōmos* (pedestal); in no known Aphrodisian inscription is a sarcophagus described as being "inside" anything, although it may be surrounded by a *topos* (place).

One illustrative example from the Southeast Necropolis consists of a well-preserved platform of large marble slabs that forms a narrow U-shape

Fig. 3.45. Abandoned sarcophagus chest near Çamarası quarry.

above and around the staircase leading down to a barrel-vaulted hypogeum, or underground chamber (fig. 3.44). A projecting lip along the inside edges of the blocks over the staircase suggests that the tomb entrance was normally covered with slabs, forming a continuous flat surface at ground level. A tier of bench blocks forms a small exedra (a monumental bench) around the tomb entrance. Along the north side of this exedra, a shallow cutting extends across the three bench blocks, indicating that something was placed on top. Measuring approximately 2.5 m wide, this cutting would be the proper size for a large sarcophagus and would provide it with a prestigious central display directly over the entrance to the tomb chamber below. This is a possible example of a *platas* supporting a *soros*, with *eisōstai* located in the underground chambers.

Sarcophagus monuments were thus major features of the Aphrodisian cemeteries and an important component of the local marble industry. The close working relationship between the quarries and the sculptural workshops in the city is demonstrated by a sarcophagus chest found near the Çamarası marble quarry, where it had been roughed out and then abandoned en route to Aphrodisias (fig. 3.45). Approximately 750 whole or fragmentary sarcophagi are known from Aphrodisias, ranging in date from the first century BC to the fourth century AD, with most falling between the first and third centuries AD. About one-fifth of the total number of known sarcophagi were first recorded by the regional survey, and these together with other sarcophagi of known provenience are of special interest for the study of the spatial evolution and social history of the cemeteries. Most of the sarcophagi recorded by the regional survey are fragmentary surface finds, and many sarcophagi were apparently reused in Late Antiquity after the plundering of the cemeteries for the construction of the City Wall.

Nevertheless, significant spatial patterns were revealed after the survey created a findspot map that shows the locations of all sarcophagi and built
tombs documented by the survey team, as well as findspots of previously
known sarcophagi (see figs. 3.41–42).

Most sarcophagi were found within the area extending 1 km from the
center of the city (excluding the city itself), which was examined with special care. Significant numbers of sarcophagi were also found immediately
outside this 1 km perimeter, even though this area was not as systematically
surveyed. Beyond a distance of about 750 m from the City Wall, however, sarcophagi are far fewer in number and more isolated. Sarcophagi
and built tombs found close to the city appear to be grouped in a series
of urban necropoleis and concentrated along paths directed toward what
would become gates in the City Wall that likely indicate the routes of
ancient roads. Positioning funerary monuments along major roads was,
of course, a traditional way for individuals and families across the Roman
Empire to display their wealth and status to passersby. Outside the urban
necropoleis only a few isolated sarcophagus finds have been documented,
often in secondary contexts. In the modern villages of Ataeymir and Seki,
for instance, sarcophagi have been built into fountains, transported there
from Aphrodisias in the early 20th century specifically for use as water
basins (fig. 3.46). In antiquity sarcophagus use seems to have been largely
an urban phenomenon, limited primarily to the necropoleis at Aphrodisias
but also seen at Bingeç, confirming the latter's special status even after the
growth of Aphrodisias.

Six necropolis areas have been identified around Aphrodisias (see fig.
3.42). The West Necropolis contains the densest concentration of chamber
tombs and sarcophagi and the most remains of aboveground tomb platforms that may have supported sarcophagi. It begins at the West Gate and
extends at least 1.2 km westward, through the area now occupied by the
modern village of Geyre. In antiquity this route was the main road into
and out of Aphrodisias, leading toward Antioch on the Maeander and
important coastal cities such as Ephesus. The North Necropolis contains
a few monuments near the Northeast and Northwest Gates and a line of

Fig. 3.46. Chest of garland sarcophagus from Aphrodisias, reused as fountain basin in modern village of Seki.

tombs extending more than 2 km northward along the road leading to ancient Attouda (modern Hisarköy). The Northeast Necropolis consists of several dense concentrations of tombs and sarcophagi outside the so-called Water Channel Gate, an area that overlaps the modern cemetery still in use by the inhabitants of Geyre. There is also a cluster of rock-cut chamber tombs farther to the northeast, along the road to the City Quarries.

The Southeast Necropolis follows the road leading from the Southeast Gate toward Herakleia Salbakes on the plain of Tabae. It contains a large number of sarcophagi but relatively few tombs and is very limited in extent, with very few remains located beyond 200 m outside the city. The South Necropolis is a much less concentrated burial area, consisting of tombs and sarcophagi dispersed throughout an area surrounding a network of roads. One road leads from the South Gate toward ancient Plarasa on the southwest plateau; another may have originally exited the city a little farther to the east on the road to Ören, where, in addition to Roman funerary remains, there is also an Ottoman cemetery and a modern *türbe*. The Southwest Necropolis follows a slightly more linear path along the road leading from the Southwest Gate, probably also toward Plarasa.

Aphrodisian sarcophagi have long been admired for their creative design and high-quality carving. The sarcophagi found during the survey correspond to well-known Aphrodisian types, including those with garland, columnar, fluted, and frieze decoration. These types are fairly evenly distributed among the necropoleis. Garland sarcophagi are by far the most numerous at Aphrodisias, constituting more than 60 percent of the total corpus of sarcophagi of known types.[39] Their production began earlier and lasted longer than the other types, extending from the late first through the late third centuries AD. Most of the survey finds belong to later styles of garland sarcophagi, dating to the second and third centuries AD, which have thicker, more elaborate fruit garlands with hanging grape clusters, supported by Nikai (images of the winged goddess of victory) on the corners and erotes on the front. Most are decorated on only three sides, with either three garland swags across the front and one on each short side or, in a variation typical to Aphrodisias, two garlands on the front framing a central panel (often inscribed) and one on each short side (see fig. 3.46). Columnar sarcophagi are the next most common type at Aphrodisias, making up about one-fourth of the total corpus.[40] Production of Aphrodisian columnar sarcophagi probably began in the mid-second century AD, inspired by the influential central Anatolian sarcophagus workshop at Dokimeion (Afyon), which produced large, very elaborate columnar sarcophagi. Only three fluted sarcophagi were documented during the survey; the largest and finest of these is located in the Northeast Necropolis and was likely made in the mid-third century AD. Frieze sarcophagi are uncommon at Aphrodisias. Those that exist are varied in theme, encompassing mythological, allegorical, and biographical subject matter; most date to the later second and early third century AD.

The evidence of inscriptions on sarcophagi for the form of tomb monuments has already been discussed. These inscriptions also provide valuable evidence for other aspects of local funerary practice. In total, 13 of the sarcophagus fragments identified by the survey bear Greek inscriptions. Although these texts are all incomplete, together they illustrate the main concerns expressed in typical Aphrodisian funerary inscriptions: concern over ownership and protection of the burial. They follow a formula common in Asia Minor, stating the name of the tomb's owner and rightful

Fig. 3.47. Sarcophagus of Aurelia Tate (third century AD), with central scene of metal-working.

occupant, the penalties for tomb violation, and sometimes details about the structure of the tomb monument and the disposition of burials within it. The threatened punishment is usually a monetary fine payable to the temple treasury or another civic body, or some other expensive obligation, such as the erection of statues of the emperors. Nevertheless, sarcophagi were frequently reused, and there are no definite records of these punishments ever being carried out. Ownership of a sarcophagus could be transferred through purchase or concession, in which case the new owner would take pains to demonstrate the legitimacy of the acquisition in the inscription. As in many tomb monuments across Asia Minor, the corpus of Aphrodisian inscriptions demonstrates an interest in family genealogy. One notable feature of the Aphrodisian inscriptions is a high incidence of the name Aurelius or its feminine, Aurelia, the *nomen* adopted by many newly enfranchised citizens in honor of the reigning imperial family following the *Constitutio Antoniniana* of Caracalla in AD 212, when citizenship was granted to all free male inhabitants of the Roman Empire (fig. 3.47).[41]

Comparisons among the necropoleis of Aphrodisias suggest social and economic characteristics that distinguish them—and therefore the people buried there—from each other. The most striking contrasts are apparent between the West and Southeast Necropoleis, which preserve the largest number of sarcophagi. Earlier, larger, and more elaborate tombs

Fig. 4.1. West side of Northeast Gate in City Wall of Aphrodisias, looking east.

building materials for the construction of the City Wall, as were the public monuments of the Agora and other areas within the city—a clear sign of the shifting priorities of the local élite and the increasing local influence of the imperial administration. The construction of fortifications must also have dramatically changed the relationship, both practical and conceptual, between the city and the countryside. It drew a much sharper boundary between urban and rural space than had ever previously existed, giving the city a new face but also restricting access (even though the major gates were apparently situated along preexisting roads) and fundamentally changing the lives of those whose houses were excluded from the fortified area (and there were surely some, even though the walls seem to have been largely wrapped around the inhabited area).

We do not know when the Temple of Aphrodite, the centerpiece of the Late Hellenistic and Augustan building program at Aphrodisias, was closed to pagan worship or first used as a Christian church. By about AD 500, at any rate, it had been dismantled and rebuilt as a huge basilica, much larger and taller than the temple it replaced—a local landmark visible for miles around (see fig. 3.2, and discussion below). This new Cathedral remained standing for half a millennium, but it was the last major building project undertaken at Late Antique Aphrodisias. Within a century, the city had been substantially abandoned, and occupation had been reduced to the areas around the Cathedral precinct and the Theater hill. By the mid-seventh century, the Theater hill had been turned into a fortified citadel—a dramatic retrenchment that may be said to mark the beginning of the Middle Ages at Aphrodisias, in which the city was returned to a state remarkably similar to that of its pre-Roman predecessor: a regional sanctuary with a relatively small associated settlement. The regional survey recorded valuable new evidence for the construction of churches and, possibly, monasteries in the countryside in Late Antiquity, as well as for changing patterns of rural settlement, helping to put the dramatic urban transformations of this period in context.

We have relatively little evidence for pre-Christian sanctuaries in the region around Aphrodisias. One clue to the sacred character of the surrounding landscape is the orientation of the Temple of Aphrodite, which departs slightly from the city grid system so as to point directly at the summit of Baba Dağı—and indeed, abundant quantities of Hellenistic and Roman fine pottery found on the top of the mountain may have been associated with some kind of peak sanctuary. Another pre-Hellenistic sanctuary discovered in the course of the survey is that of Meter Adrastou, apparently just across the northern border of the territory of Aphrodisias, in the region of the neighboring city of Attouda at Taşoluk Mevkii (discussed below in the context of the Early Christian sanctuary at the same site). Many of the architectural fragments identified in the course of the survey may have been associated with shrines, but they could also have belonged to rural villas or monumental tombs. So while the region around Aphrodisias was surely filled with sacred springs and groves and other ritual sites, the pagan religious map of the region remains largely blank to us today.

Christianization of the Landscape (by Örgü Dalgıç)

The sacred landscape of the region becomes more visible after its Christianization, in part because a number of both rural and suburban churches were maintained into the Middle Ages and are therefore better preserved today than their pagan predecessors. The earliest records of Christianity at Aphrodisias relate to two local Christian men martyred in the city in the later third century.[42] The earliest documented bishop of Aphrodisias appears in the fourth century, when a certain Ammonius participated in and signed the acts of the Council of Nicaea in AD 325. From the late fourth century onward, Christians were represented in almost all social classes, but it is only in the late fifth and early sixth century, when the Temple of Aphrodite was converted into the Cathedral, that substantial numbers of inscriptions are found honoring various local Christian bene-factors or commemorating the Christian deceased. Until this time con-servative pagans apparently maintained a significant constituency among the wealthy and higher-ranking members of society. There is evidence that pagan sacrifices continued to be made through the 480s, and it is at about this time that evidence appears of active hostilities by Christians against remaining pagan groups.[43] Considering the strength of the pagan upper class, it is possible that the Temple of Aphrodite remained under their control until at least the third quarter of the fifth century or even possibly until the early sixth century.

The transformation of the Temple into the Cathedral marks a water-shed in the status of Christianity in the city, presumably brought about by the conversion of a critical mass of the local aristocracy, or by the initiative of a powerful bishop, or by a combination of these and other factors. The roof and upper entablature of the Temple as well as the ashlar walls of the cella were taken down. The columns of the east and west façades were also dis-mantled and then reerected to extend the lines of the undisturbed north and south colonnades of the peristyle; these became the colonnades of the nave of the new basilical church, with a clerestory rising on top of the columns. The reerected columns stood on foundations made of reused entablature blocks, and the blocks of the cella walls were used in the lowest courses of the outer walls of the new church. The orientation of the building was reversed, with a new atrium built on the west side and an apse to the east. The new building was much larger than the old one and extended far enough to the east that the new altar and synthronon (seating for the clergy) may have covered the site of the former sacred spring and altar to Aphrodite. The Late Hellenistic

Temple of Aphrodite had not been especially large at approximately 18.5 m by 32 m. The new Cathedral, about 31 m by 72 m, dwarfed the memory of the old building, and because of the clerestory it was also much taller. It was the most conspicuous feature of the Late Antique skyline.

Until recently the only ecclesiastical buildings known in the city were the Cathedral and a Medieval Triconch Church (discussed in the next chapter). The regional survey located evidence for as many as 17 Christian monuments in the surrounding territory, both in the immediate environs of the city and in the hinterland (fig. 4.2). Three or possibly four churches are situated just outside the main gates of the City Wall in the area of the cemeteries that lined the main roads leading into the city (fig. 4.3). Other churches are scattered through the countryside, and on the evidence of location and date, they fall into three general groups: Early Christian (fourth to sixth century AD) buildings on the floor of the Morsynus valley; Middle Byzantine (ninth to 11th century AD) chapels in the hills to the north and south of the valley (discussed in the next chapter); and a mixture of earlier and later structures on the plateau to the southwest.

Of special interest are the three or possibly four churches immediately outside the City Wall of Aphrodisias, some or all of which may have been built near the tombs of local Christian martyrs or holy men and women. These extramural churches were discovered during the intensive survey of the immediate environs of Aphrodisias, and each has been named after the nearest gate of the City Wall.

The West Church is the largest and best preserved, located only about 50 m outside the City Wall, just to the south of the West Gate, on the south side of the road that connected Aphrodisias with the Maeander River valley to the northwest (see fig. 4.3). The church lies within the extensive West Necropolis, and some of the Roman tombs found nearby certainly continued to be used through the Early Christian period. As preserved, the church is a three-aisled basilica with a central dome and vaulted aisles dating most probably to the late ninth or early 10th century AD, making it the only extramural church of the Middle Byzantine period

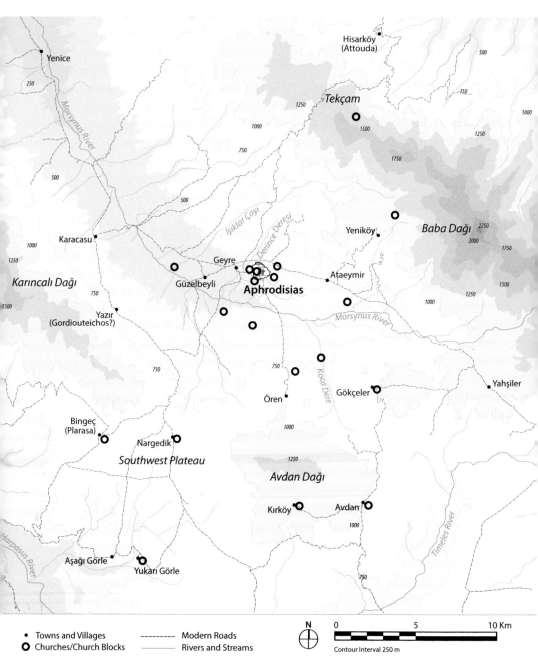

Fig. 4.2. Map of Aphrodisias survey region, showing locations of churches and related architectural blocks.

Fig. 4.3. Satellite image showing locations of extramural churches.

(fig. 4.4). However, the current remains seem to belong to a second phase of construction that replaced an Early Christian basilica. While details of the construction of the Middle Byzantine phase are treated in the next chapter, some aspects of the proposed Early Christian phase can be reconstructed from the standing remains.

The building measures approximately 22 m (north–south) by 35 m (east–west) including the narthex (L: 22 m; W: 4.3 m) and single large apse (Diam: 8.3 m), which, together with two rectilinear side chambers,

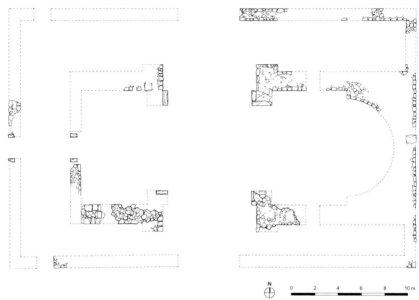

Fig. 4.4. Plan of West Church.

is entirely contained within the rectangular outline of the building. The walls that define the outer shell of the structure are 0.75 m thick and built of irregularly coursed, heavily mortared masonry. In contrast, the 1.65-m-thick interior walls are much more substantial. They are bonded with four articulated piers, constructed of mortared rubble faced with ashlar blocks probably all recycled from earlier Roman structures. These piers clearly carried massive arches, which spanned the nave and aisles and supported a large central dome 7.3 m in diameter over the central bay of the nave. Both sets of doorjambs at the western entrance are preserved, and those leading from the narthex to the nave are still standing (fig. 4.5).

While the more substantial interior walls indicate that the present structure was domed and vaulted, the outer shell suggests an originally lighter building, possibly a basilical church with a wooden roof. A composite capital (preserved H: 0.55 m; W at top: 0.73 m) found inside the nave directly in front of the entrance from the narthex (fig. 4.6), as well as double-engaged

Fig. 4.5. Southwest dome pier and standing narthex   Fig. 4.6. Capital from West Church.
doorjambs of West Church, looking northwest.

capitals found reused as mullions in the broad north and south windows, could all be remnants of the earlier building. A second indicator of an Early Christian initial construction date is the form of the east end of the church. The way the central apse and side rooms are inscribed within—rather than projecting from—the rectangular plan of the building is an unusual detail this church shares with the Cathedral. This so-called Syrian type of east end is found in other early basilicas throughout western Asia Minor, all with construction dates between the fourth and sixth centuries, and may therefore reflect the design of an earlier building on the same site.[44] Indeed, it would not be surprising if a church had occupied this site, just outside the major gate of the city and on the edge of a time-honored cemetery, in the fifth or sixth century or even earlier. Additionally, evidence suggests that an important Christian site existed outside the West Gate before the ninth century since the outer face of the City Wall and the walls of the gate passage are covered with inscribed crosses, some of which were hidden below a Middle Byzantine repaving of the road through the gate.[45] The location outside a gate and within a major necropolis is an obvious site for a martyrion, and this initial church could perhaps be associated with the Middle Byzantine martyrion "dedicated to the holy martyrs Barbara and Anastasia" known from an inscribed lintel block now in the Aphrodisias Museum.[46]

Another of the recently discovered extramural churches, the Northeast Church, is situated along the ancient road leading from the Northeast Gate

Fig. 4.7. Plan of
Northeast Church.

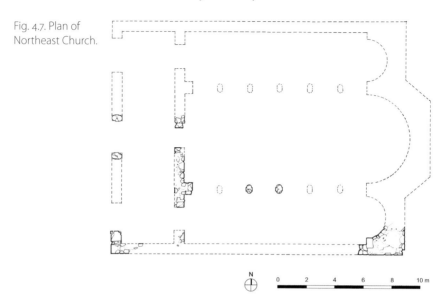

Fig. 4.7. Plan of
Northeast Church.

out toward the City Quarries, about 500 m northeast of the Northeast Gate
and about 150 m north of a concentration of Late Antique tombs (see fig.
4.3). This site, immediately south of the Karacasu-Tavas highway, now lies
within the modern cemetery of the old village of Geyre, which occupies
part of the ancient Northeast Necropolis of Aphrodisias. The Northeast
Church appears to have a three-aisled basilica plan with a narthex to the
west and a triple-apsed sanctuary to the east (fig. 4.7). With overall exterior
dimensions of approximately 16 m (north–south) by 22.5 m (east–west),
this is the smallest of the newly discovered extramural churches. Very little
of the mortared rubble walls is visible above present ground level; where
measurable, the walls are a uniform thickness of 0.70 m.

A pair of in-situ double-engaged column bases are used as doorjambs
for a doorway that marks the main entrance to the narthex of the church.
A second doorway in the eastern wall of the narthex, aligned with the west
doorway, marks the entrance from the narthex to the nave. The eastern
narthex wall is visible on both sides and better preserved toward the south,
where a second doorway interrupts the wall; a third doorway restored
to the north would provide a triple entrance to the nave and side aisles

from the narthex. An engaged pier between the central and the southern doorways marks the west end of the south colonnade. Aligned with that pier, the bases of two of the columns of the south colonnade remain in situ. They are bases for double-engaged columns and are spaced 1.30 m apart, allowing for a five-column colonnade between the central nave and each of the side aisles. Not coincidentally, many of the headstones used in the modern cemetery around the church are repurposed double-engaged half-columns, carved out of the mottled gray marble found at the quarry near Yazır. The general plan of the east end of the building is preserved as a crescent-shaped rubble mound extending 4 m farther east beyond the preserved southeast corner of the building, perhaps marking the collapsed semidome over the central apse. The plan of the Northeast Church is of a standard basilica type: the nave and aisles are divided by rows of columns, and each terminates in a semicircular apse to the east. This plan finds numerous parallels dated to the fifth and sixth centuries AD, especially in Asia Minor and Cyprus. Four octagonal floor tiles (0.26 m by 0.26 m) found scattered around a robber's pit near the east end of the nave are similar to tiles found throughout the city in floors that are mostly Late Antique or Early Byzantine in date.

It is possible that, like the West Church, the Northeast Church was also a martyrion. The Northeast Necropolis is host to the most tightly packed cluster of built tombs among all the necropoleis of Aphrodisias. Over the doorway to one of the many chamber tombs here, about 150 m south of the Northeast Church, an inscribed lintel block names the tomb as that of the bishop Theopropius: A *chi-rho* Ω Θεοπροπ[ίο]υ *leaf* A *chi-rho* Ω Ζῆ ἐπισκ[όπο]υ; "(Tomb) of Theopropius, the bishop. Still alive." The inscription has been dated to the mid-fifth century; Theopropius may even have been a bishop of Aphrodisias.[47] The mid-fifth-century date of the tomb suggests that the church, or at least a shrine, may have already existed in the area during this period. The presence of a bishop's tomb suggests that the tombs contiguous with it were intended for Christian burial as well, and that in the mid-fifth century the Northeast Necropolis may have been a preferred site of burial for Aphrodisian Christians.

Fig. 4.8. Southwest Church, looking east.   Fig. 4.9. Capital with cross
from Southwest Church.

Understanding the Northeast Church as a martyrion would help explain the popularity of this cemetery among members of the city's Early Christian community.

A third extramural church, the Southwest Church, is located about 250 m outside the City Wall, and the ruins rest nearly on top of an earlier Roman tomb in the Southwest Necropolis (see fig. 4.3). A mound of rubble and scattered architectural blocks and piles of fieldstones from the surrounding area measure approximately 30 m (east–west) by 17 m (north–south) (fig. 4.8). The church is not well preserved, but it is oriented east–west and appears to also follow a basilica plan, probably with three aisles and a large central apse. Among the strewn architectural blocks are two composite capitals, dating to the High Roman Imperial period and similar to the one at the West Church, except that one of the capitals is reworked with crosses in place of the fleuron on two opposing faces (H: 0.55 m; W at top: 0.73 m) (fig. 4.9).

Immediately outside and south of the Southeast Gate, the second most important entrance after the West Gate, are three standing marble architectural elements (a doorjamb and two columns) that could indicate the presence of another extramural church (see fig. 4.3). Although no traces of walls are visible, the locations of the three known extramural churches support this interpretation, as does the high concentration of Christian inscriptions and graffiti on the City Wall to both the north and south of the gate.[48]

In addition to these extramural churches, a number of both Early Christian and Middle Byzantine structures have been identified in the surrounding countryside. Middle Byzantine buildings in the countryside are located in the remote hills to the north (near Yeniköy) and south (just north of Ören), and on the southwest plateau (near Görle, Nargedik, and Avdan). These structures, along with Middle Byzantine activity at Aphrodisias itself, represent the settlement habits of the population in the early Medieval period and will be discussed in the next chapter. By contrast, the Early Christian rural churches are dispersed across the valley floor and located at the sites of the earlier towns of Bingeç (ancient Plarasa) and Yukarı Görle on the southwest plateau. An exception to this pattern is the Early Christian building at Taşoluk (near Tekçam, on the northern border of the survey area). It is interesting to note that evidence for both Early Christian and Middle Byzantine building activity within the same site was found at only two places: at Aphrodisias itself (the Cathedral and the extramural West Church), and at Yukarı Görle, which, like Bingeç, was the site of a significant settlement in the Hellenistic period.

Material evidence for these rural church buildings varies from site to site. In some cases, the outlines of small churches or chapels are preserved on the ground, while other churches are suggested by isolated but distinctive architectural elements, such as an ambo platform or a decorated epistyle block. Other blocks, such as screen panels, are less architecturally definitive and need not indicate a church per se but rather a monumental structure with a Christian sponsor. Often these decontextualized fragments can be associated with a nearby site. Occasionally, as at Bingeç and Yukarı Görle on the southwest plateau (figs. 4.10–11), Christian blocks are used as spolia built into the walls of modern village houses and therefore cannot be associated with any specific original location; however, they remain indicative of a church or other Christian building somewhere in the vicinity.

The functions of the different Christian sites cannot be securely determined, but they must have served small rural congregations, whether based

Fig. 4.10. Impost capital with Maltese cross at Bingeç.

Fig. 4.11. Two screen panels, with other large marble blocks, built into village house at Yukarı Görle.

at independent settlements, villas, or monasteries. Literary sources document monasteries in the territory of Aphrodisias, and one of the sites identified by the survey, Kocadere, has some of the characteristics of a monastic installation. The site is situated 6 km southeast of Aphrodisias at 650 masl atop a fairly level natural terrace above the left (west) bank of the seasonal Koca Dere (see fig. 4.2; fig. 4.12). The complex seems to comprise a walled precinct with a substantial building at the center and a number of subsidiary buildings round about. A dense layer of tile, brick, pithos, and pottery fragments blankets the site, and a number of agricultural processing blocks may be associated with the production of olive oil. Pottery collected at the site dates the complex securely to the Late Antique period and shows that primary occupation ended by the seventh to eighth century (but continued in some fashion into the Middle Byzantine period). An ambo platform and a fragment of a marble basin were found on the terrace south of the mound occupying the center of the site (fig. 4.13). The ambo platform (L: 1.25 m; W: 1.00 m; D: 0.22 m) is a round slab, with two rectangular projections on opposite sides (W: 0.74 m). The edges of the round central part are beveled, and the ends of the projections are unfinished or possibly broken. On the underside is a round recessed soffit (Diam: 0.74 m), within which is carved a cross with enlarged termini in low relief (L: 0.45 m; W: 0.40 m).

The ambo platform served as the floor of the ambo, the pulpit or elevated speaker's platform in a church, which was usually located toward the center of the nave (fig. 4.14). Two more ambo platforms were found at

Fig. 4.12. View of Kocadere monastery site, looking east.

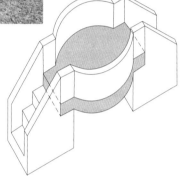

Fig. 4.13. Ambo platform from Kocadere monastery.

Fig. 4.14. Schematic drawing of Early Christian ambo, with platform highlighted in gray.

other sites in the region, at Geyre and Taşoluk (see below, fig. 4.18). All the platforms belong to the same type of ambo, which had a central circular body and two stairways on opposite sides, one leading toward the clergy in the apse and one toward the congregation in the nave. All three of the ambo platforms recorded by the survey have molded profiles, and their soffits have concave circular depressions, as noted above. In the case of the Kocadere and Geyre platforms, the circular depression is inscribed with a cross in low relief. In western Caria, the prevailing type of ambo platform is octagonal rather than circular. Most examples of circular ambo platforms like those found around Aphrodisias are from the Aegean Islands and are dated to the sixth century AD.

Fig. 4.15. Taşoluk, view across site toward Maeander River valley, looking northeast.

As at Kocadere, the ambo platform found at Taşoluk indicates the presence of a nearby church, possibly associated with a monastery. The site of Taşoluk, however, does not fit the pattern of Early Christian monuments in the valley and Middle Byzantine monuments in the hills. It sits high on the ridge northeast of Aphrodisias at nearly 1,400 masl, in a well-watered natural terrace overlooking the Maeander River valley, just northeast of Tekçam, the pass that crosses the Baba Dağı Ridge on the road from the Morsynus River valley to ancient Attouda (modern Hisarköy) (see fig. 4.2; fig. 4.15). What is more, the Early Christian sanctuary at Taşoluk appears to have been built on the site of the earlier sanctuary of Meter Adrastou, one of the most prominent pagan cults at Attouda (the name of the goddess, Meter, is accompanied by a divine epithet consisting of the personal name of the cult founder, Adrastos).[49] The survey recorded three important blocks associated with the sanctuary in two houses in the modern village of Ataköy (see fig. 4.2). One block is a screen post with an integral base for a colonette; the second is a panel carved in shallow relief with a tall cross; and the third is inscribed with a dedication to the goddess Meter Adrastou (fig. 4.16). All three blocks were said to have been brought there from a "ruined church" at Taşoluk, roughly 10 km away as the crow flies. At Taşoluk itself, the survey recorded a dense scatter of sherds and roof tiles, as well as numerous

Fig. 4.16. Fragmentary block with dedication to Meter Adrastou, built into village house near Ataköy.

architectural elements. Some of the worked blocks that bore clamp cuttings and anathyrosis, including orthostats and cornices, should be Hellenistic or Early Roman, and the pottery suggests this phase should be dated to the first century BC or AD. In this period, a substantial structure must have been built here, likely a temple or shrine situated near an abundant spring that still waters the site. The temple or shrine was dedicated to Meter Adrastou, the chief deity of Attouda, as indicated by the votive inscription moved from Taşoluk to Ataköy. The site therefore likely lay outside the territory of Aphrodisias, and the crest of the ridge marked the border between the territories of the two cities.

A second monumental phase at the site of Taşoluk is indicated by architectural elements that clearly belonged to an Early Christian church. These include two screen panels identical to the one recorded at Ataköy, one of which is reused in the fountain basin of the spring on the terrace (fig. 4.17), and a circular ambo platform, broken in two, with molded profile and rectangular projections on opposite sides (fig. 4.18). These elements, as well as smaller columns, pedestal bases, and double capitals, can be dated roughly to the late fifth or early sixth century AD. The transformation of the sanctuary at Taşoluk from a pagan religious site to a Christian church is thus the rural equivalent, in the territory of Attouda, of the conversion of the Temple of Aphrodite at Aphrodisias into the Cathedral around or before AD 500.

Fig. 4.17. Cross panel reused in fountain   Fig. 4.18. Ambo platform from Taşoluk.
basin at Taşoluk.

Early Christianity in the territory is thus evident both in urban centers—such as Aphrodisias itself, as well as Bingeç and Yukarı Görle on the southwest plateau—and in the countryside, in the form of two sites in isolated locations that seem to have been monasteries, and chapels near or belonging to country estates owned by the local élite. These rural sites can all be dated to the late fifth to sixth centuries on the evidence of pottery, architectural elements, or inscriptions, which suggests that the Christianization of the countryside was more or less contemporary with that of the towns. The few instances where there is explicit evidence for monumental Christian structures or churches suggest that the élite played an instrumental role in bringing the church to the countryside at about the same time as the conversion of the Temple of Aphrodite at Aphrodisias. We know, for example, from the *Life of Severus*, a saint's biography that dates to the late fifth century, that the founders of the first monastery near Aphrodisias were indeed two local aristocrats, the brothers Paralius and Athanasius. They converted to monophysite Christianity while studying in Alexandria and returned to Aphrodisias in the 490s as eager missionaries, founding a monastery and converting many local pagans.

Late Antique Settlement

Though the Christianization of the countryside as revealed by monumental architectural remains is evident at relatively few sites, the number of

Late Antique habitation sites recorded in the survey area suggests that the countryside of Aphrodisias remained occupied through the Late Antique period, and the intensity of agricultural activity attests continued rural wealth and prosperity. On the valley floor, Late Antique settlement consists mostly of farmsteads, some of which contain, in addition to agricultural blocks, clusters of isolated architectural elements of Roman or Late Antique date that may originate from monumental tombs. These more elaborate farmsteads seem to have been villa-like monumental rural residences of the local aristocracy, and some have clear signs of Christian activity. It is not difficult to imagine cases in which a wealthy aristocrat sponsored the construction of a small church or chapel on or near his country estate. In the hills to the north and south of Aphrodisias, types of Late Antique habitation range from extensive settlements to farmsteads to the possible monastery at Kocadere, as already noted. But besides this monastery, which does not lie precisely in the hills but rather on the edge of the valley floor, there are no other clear signs of Early Christian structures in the hills.

Occupation on the southwest plateau apparently was never as intensive as that on the valley floor and in the surrounding hills, but it continued unbroken through Late Antiquity. Two major ancient towns on the southwest plateau were Plarasa at modern Bingeç and an as yet unidentified settlement at modern Yukarı Görle, and Christian presence is evident at both sites. The four other ancient settlements recorded on the plateau are identified as fortified farms or olive oil factories, two site types that are found only here, and not on the valley floor or surrounding hills. At none of these extensive rural settlements did we encounter churches or other overt signs of Christianity. The most substantial settlement is located at Koca Ören, 1.5 km east of the modern village of Tekeliler (see fig. 3.11). It can be interpreted as an olive oil factory associated either with a large estate or with a village whose collective economy was based on olive oil production. The settlement consists of at least 30 small rooms surrounding a large cistern and the remains of at least 11 presses, which alone could have supplied approximately 13 to 25 percent of the valley's entire population with each annual

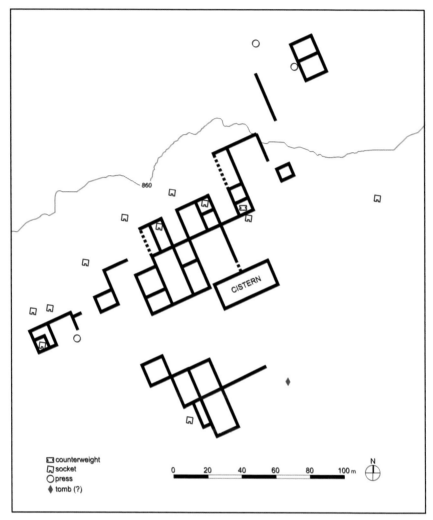

Fig. 4.19. Plan of Koca Ören olive oil "factory."

harvest (figs. 4.19–20).[50] Factories such as this one suggest that investment in agricultural production became more intensive during the later Roman Imperial period, continuing into Late Antiquity, with the establishment of monastic communities that were also equipped with press installations, such as the Kocadere monastery, noted above.

Fig. 4.20. Cistern at Koca Ören, looking northeast.

Although Aphrodisias enjoyed a period of relative prosperity during the mid-fourth to mid-sixth century, attested by major building projects such as the construction of the City Wall and the conversion of the Temple, the seventh century witnessed the first significant decrease in urban population, along with the collapse of major buildings that were never reerected. The large-scale abandonment of Aphrodisias is representative of the dramatic changes that took place across much of Asia Minor by the mid-seventh century, including widespread depopulation, the breakdown of long-distance trade, and a decline in the quantity and quality of material goods. Long considered to mark a "Dark Age," the effects of these changes were felt variously across the diminished Early Byzantine state. During this transitional period, many features of Graeco-Roman society were abandoned, and new forms of settlement, economic activity, and social organization grew in their place.

One of the major questions asked at the beginning of the survey concerned the relationship between the large-scale abandonment of Aphrodisias in the early seventh century and rural settlement. Was the city abandoned because of a local catastrophe, such as an earthquake, plague, or foreign invasion? Or was the abandonment part of a more general systemic collapse of the Roman provincial system, and of the administrative network that had encouraged the populations of rural areas such as this one to live in towns instead of villages, by maintaining the infrastructure of rural roads, waterworks, and other amenities that made town life possible in the first place? What happened to the people when the city was abandoned? Was there a catastrophic increase in mortality? Or did the population simply melt back into the countryside from which their ancestors had come many centuries before?

As we have seen, settlement before the founding of the city in the second century BC appears to have been concentrated in the surrounding hills, and it would not have been surprising if this pre-Roman pattern had reasserted itself at the end of Late Antiquity (as was apparently the case within the city of Aphrodisias itself). But that does not seem to have been the case. The sites abandoned in the Imperial period do not appear to have been reoccupied (with the exception of the possible monastery at Kocadere, founded near the site of a Late Hellenistic and Early Imperial settlement), and a number of sites occupied into the fourth or fifth century were abandoned at that time. Reconstructions of ancient settlement patterns based on data collected by surveys such as ours are inevitably patchy and incomplete, but at least we can say that in the region around Aphrodisias, we have not found evidence for an increase in rural population corresponding to the decrease in urban population at the end of Late Antiquity. On the contrary, both the urban and the rural populations seem to have gone into decline at about the same time. And we have found very little recognizable evidence for habitation in the countryside after the seventh century.

On this evidence, the large-scale abandonment of Aphrodisias in the early seventh century does not seem to represent simply a dramatic change in settlement pattern, in which a relatively stable regional population redistributed itself differently across the landscape. Rather, it appears to mark a real and significant reduction in population. This reduction could be the result of a variety of factors, including increased mortality and migration. It could be the result of a declining birth rate and lower life expectancy that had been building up for generations. In any case, it is worth remarking that of the classic explanations for the collapse of the populations of towns like Aphrodisias, the only one that would have produced a sudden and significant increase in mortality, especially in urban populations, is plague. It is difficult, however, to determine how rapidly the process of abandonment unfolded—whether it took place all at once, precipitated by something like the plague, or over the course of two or three generations, as the civic institutions that had made the Graeco-Roman city attractive in the first place gradually deteriorated, encouraging inhabitants to move elsewhere.

While the exact settlement pattern of the Late Hellenistic and Early Imperial periods in the Morsynus River valley does not reassert itself at the end of Late Antiquity, there are interesting similarities between the earlier Hellenistic and the Medieval settlement patterns in the survey region as a whole, for the plateau southwest of Aphrodisias has a different history from that of the Morsynus River valley. While the population of the plateau does not seem to have experienced the same kind of increase in the Roman period as the population of the valley, neither did it witness the same kind of decline in Late Antiquity. It is as if the great explosion of the Roman Empire—with the exception of olive cultivation in Late Antiquity, as noted above—largely passed it by. The southwest plateau did not have the advantages—water supply, soil fertility, accessibility—that made the remarkable development of the valley possible during the Roman Peace. But it could and possibly did maintain the same level of population in the so-called Dark and Middle Ages as it had in pre-Roman times, when the accessibility of the valley was a disadvantage rather than an advantage.

5 THE MIDDLE BYZANTINE REVIVAL
(Angela Commito and Örgü Dalgıç)

Like many towns across Asia Minor, Aphrodisias remained occupied on a reduced scale throughout the early Medieval period and seems to have enjoyed something of a Renaissance in the Middle Byzantine era. The city came to be known as Stauropolis—"City of the Cross"—and eventually as Caria. Recent excavations in the area between the Temple and the Theater show continued habitation up to the early seventh century, and then sudden and total abandonment. Houses and major buildings such as the Sebasteion, Theater stage building, Agora Gate, and Civil Basilica collapsed and were never rebuilt. The seventh century therefore marks a dramatic retrenchment both of the cityscape and of the population of Aphrodisias at the end of Late Antiquity.

But the city lived on, in altered form: in the 10th century Aphrodisias was still the seat of the metropolitan bishopric of Caria, and still served as a focal point of settlement and economic activity, now largely driven and organized by the episcopal administration, as the role of the bishop grew to supplant traditional Graeco-Roman civic institutions. Dense occupation in the city was perhaps limited to the area between the Theater hill and the Cathedral, but this small community must have been somewhat vibrant in the Middle Byzantine period. Not only was it the seat of the metropolitan bishopric, but there was new construction as well, in the form of a small Triconch Church built over a major street southwest of the Theater hill, incorporating a four-column monument at the intersection (see fig. 3.1).

The clearest indication of renewed prosperity in the Middle Byzantine period is the refurbishment of the Cathedral. Major changes were made at the east end, where a new sanctuary screen was installed, and the walls of the tunnel below the synthronon were painted with frescoes dated stylistically to the late 10th or 11th century. New floors were laid throughout the Cathedral, which also received new marble furnishings, and a pavement was placed in the area of the surrounding temenos enclosure, where a large cemetery was also created. The cemetery extended beyond the temenos to the east in the original forecourt of the Sanctuary of Aphrodite and southward toward the Bouleuterion. An olive and perhaps also a wine press were built up against the back wall of Bouleuterion, and the area east of the Bouleuterion may have been used for commerce or food distribution. On the west side of the Bouleuterion, a large Late Antique house was renovated and expanded in the 10th or 11th century; none of the other known Late Antique houses in the city were similarly refurbished and reoccupied. Given its proximity to the Cathedral and its interior decoration, including images of what may be angels (the cult of the archangel Michael was very important at Aphrodisias, and the Cathedral was likely dedicated to him), the so-called Bishop's Palace complex likely served as the headquarters of the bishop and his staff. All the lead seals from Aphrodisias with recorded find locations (14 of 17 in total) come from this structure—these include seven bishops' seals (eighth to 11th century) and seven seals of imperial officials or dignitaries (eighth to 10th century). The Bishop's Palace was not simply a residence but rather the multifunctional heart of the ecclesiastical administration and economic life of the town. Here the bishop would have lived and worked but also received audiences and overseen the collection, processing, and distribution of agricultural products.[51]

A second major area of habitation in Middle Byzantine Aphrodisias was the Theater hill, which served as a fortified citadel for the settlement. The Theater stage building had collapsed during the seventh century, and fortification walls were erected around the slopes of the hill and against the east face of the collapsed stage building at some point during the later 10th to 12th century. Houses were constructed over debris in the Theater cavea.

Another focal point of activity in the Middle Byzantine settlement was the West Church, located just outside the West Gate of the City Wall, which had partly collapsed at this time and was no longer a dependable means of defense.[52] The West Church was rebuilt as a domed basilica, an architectural type common in the late ninth and early 10th centuries (see discussion in chapter 4, with figures). As noted above, this church could perhaps be the Middle Byzantine martyrion "dedicated to the holy martyrs Barbara and Anastasia" known from an inscribed lintel block now in the Aphrodisias Museum.[53] Also in the Middle Byzantine period, the road through the West Gate was repaved over a layer of large blocks that had fallen from the superstructure and were not moved aside.[54] The rebuilding of the church and the clearing of the gate may have been concurrent, as it is clear that the gate and road were active in connecting the rebuilt West Church to the Cathedral precinct and city center. Beyond these practical considerations, the symbolic significance of the dome in Middle Byzantine ecclesiastical architecture may have provided another impetus for the renovation of an earlier church on this site, as it was the driving force behind the reconfiguration of many already monumental churches as domed basilicas in the late ninth to early 10th century across Asia Minor and Thrace.[55] The rebuilding of the West Church as a domed basilica and the remains of what might be another extramural church outside the Southeast Gate suggest these locations as centers of satellite communities located alongside agricultural land, but also close enough to the fortified part of the city to offer security.

In some regions of Asia Minor, large-scale abandonment of city centers by the seventh century did not go hand in hand with wholesale depopulation of the countryside. Survey projects have demonstrated that in some places, rural settlement continued to a varied degree throughout the so-called Dark Age of the seventh and eighth centuries.[56] The countryside around Aphrodisias, however, seems to have suffered along with the city. Our survey did not reveal evidence of habitation in the countryside in the seventh to ninth centuries, though our lack of understanding of the ceramics of this period may make the picture appear darker than it truly was. Such evidence reemerges only in the 10th and 11th centuries, and it is sparsely scatted over a wide territory. As noted in the preceding chapter, Middle Byzantine buildings in the countryside are located in the remote hills to the north at Yeniköy and to the south at Başbaş near Ören, and on the southwest plateau (see fig. 4.2).

The chapel on a hill above Yeniköy is a small, single-nave structure with the apse toward the east and perhaps a narthex toward the west (fig.

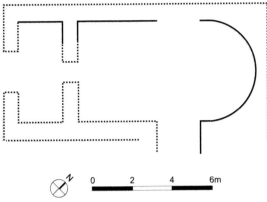

Fig. 5.2. Jamb block with interlace pattern from Yeniköy chapel.

Fig. 5.1. Plan of Yeniköy chapel.

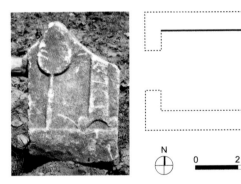

Fig. 5.3. Panel with cypress and cross from Yeniköy chapel.

Fig. 5.4. Plan of Başbaş chapel.

5.1). Remains of the collapsed vault or semidome of the building cover the extant walls, and fragments of the church's marble decoration were found nearby. The design of a doorjamb block, with interlocked chains of guilloches and lozenges, is comparable to the architectural decoration of the refurbished Cathedral in Aphrodisias, dated to the 10th century (fig. 5.2). A fragment of a screen panel contains the lower arm of a lobed cross and a stylized cypress tree, motifs well known from Late Antiquity through the Middle Ages (fig. 5.3). The chapel at Başbaş, situated on a hillside across the valley floor from Yeniköy about 7 km south of Aphrodisias, is of slightly smaller dimensions and consists of a single nave with an apse at its east end (fig. 5.4). A number of marble architectural blocks were

Fig. 5.5. Epistyle block from Başbaş chapel.   Fig. 5.6. Epistyle block from Başbaş chapel.

found in the area, including three epistyle fragments, two carved with a motif of three rows of tangent and intersecting circles overlapping to form four-petaled flowers, and one decorated with a row of palmettes inscribed within incomplete tangent circles (figs. 5.5–6). Similar motifs are found in 11th- to 12th-century churches elsewhere in Asia Minor.[57] Small hillside chapels like these, built of rudimentarily coursed mortared rubble, with simple plans consisting of an apse, a nave, and a narthex, are common in Asia Minor from the sixth to the 13th century.[58] The church at Yeniköy is associated with a preexisting Roman cemetery, and agricultural blocks are scattered in the areas around both churches. The lack of substantial remains of settlements or large estates suggests that these churches served small rural communities sited to take advantage of more remote agricultural lands, which may have been considered relatively safe in contrast to the valley floor. The historically defensive position of both sites is highlighted by the presence of pre-Roman citadels in the hills above both locations, at Yeniköy and Ören (see chapter 2).

Additional isolated fragments of typically Middle Byzantine (particularly 11th-century) architectural sculpture that were likely part of the liturgical furnishings of rural church buildings are built into the walls of modern village houses across the southwest plateau. These blocks include an epistyle block decorated with a guilloche and a griffin at Nargedik (fig. 5.7), a marble colonette and a fragment of an unusual yellow limestone screen panel decorated with geometric motifs at Avdan (fig. 5.8), and a marble altar decorated with a cross at Kırköy. That the early Christian

Fig. 5.7. Epistyle block with guilloche and griffin built into village house at Nargedik.

Fig. 5.8. Limestone panel with spiral and floral motifs, with Ottoman headstone, built into village house at Avdan.

community in evidence at Yukarı Görle survived through the Middle Byzantine period is indicated by the redecoration of some rock-cut tombs in an extensive Hellenistic or Early Roman necropolis that extends across the base of the cliffs north of the village. One of the tombs, consisting of an antechamber followed by a main chamber with two couches along the side walls, was frescoed in the Middle Byzantine period. The best-preserved section of the fresco is in the southeast quarter of the main chamber and shows two frontal, haloed figures with individualized features (fig. 5.9). The larger figure is the Virgin Mary and the smaller, unidentified

Fig. 5.9. Painted tomb at Yukarı Görle.

figure may perhaps be a martyr since he holds a cross in his right hand in front of his chest. The fragmentary frescoes cannot be dated definitively, but the style of painting may indicate a ninth- or 10th-century date.[59]

As noted in the previous chapter, evidence of both Early Christian and Middle Byzantine building activity within the same site was found at only two places: at Aphrodisias itself and at Yukarı Görle, which, like Bingeç, was the site of a significant settlement on the southwest plateau in the Hellenistic period. Although both Bingeç and Görle contain reused Early Christian architectural elements suggesting the presence of churches nearby, only at Görle is there evidence for activity in the Middle Byzantine period as well.

The renovation of the Cathedral and West Church and the construction of the Triconch Church at Aphrodisias, the construction of rural chapels in the hills at Yeniköy and Başbaş, and the frescoed tomb at Yukarı Görle on the southwest plateau are emblematic of the revival of the 10th and 11th centuries. This era of growing prosperity was cut short, however, by the depopulation of Aphrodisias as a result of continuous conflict between the Byzantine state and the Seljuk Turks, who succeeded in taking over the Anatolian peninsula one and one-quarter centuries after their victory over Byzantine forces at the Battle of Manzikert (Malazgirt) in AD 1071. Aphrodisias was located in an area strategic to the ongoing Byzantine-Seljuk clashes of the late 11th through 13th centuries and was captured by the Seljuk forces at least four times between 1080 and 1260. Emblematic of these changes is the fate of the refurbished Cathedral: not long after its Middle Byzantine renovations, the building was destroyed by fire around AD 1200 and never rebuilt.

6 FROM THE SELJUK CONQUEST TO THE PRESENT DAY

In AD 1196 or 1197, according to the Byzantine historian Nicetas Choniates, the Seljuk sultan of Iconium, Kaykhusraw I, fell upon the town of Caria, together with the neighboring community of Tantalus, and deported their inhabitants, some 5,000 in total, to Philomelium in Phrygia.[60] Caria was the Byzantine name of Aphrodisias, and Tantalus may be associated with a flat-topped hill, crowned by a Byzantine citadel, located near the modern town of Dandalas (see fig. 1.12). Just under a decade earlier, in 1188 or 1189, a Byzantine royal pretender, Theodore Mangaphas, had also attacked the town of Caria with the support of the same Kaykhusraw and burned the church of St. Michael, presumably the refurbished Cathedral.[61] These twin assaults, the first significant military operations known to us in the Morsynus River valley for many centuries, signal the end of the Byzantine and the beginning of the Turkish period in the area around Aphrodisias.

Choniates uses the term *komopolis*—a compound of *kome*, meaning village, and *polis*, meaning city—to describe both Caria and Tantalus. The figure he gives of 5,000 for their combined population is interestingly large, considering that our estimates of the population of Roman Aphrodisias run from 6,500 to 12,500 persons, and it suggests that the Middle Byzantine revival of the city was accompanied by a considerable revival of the rural economy as well. Nevertheless, the life of a peasant on the borders of the Middle Byzantine state must have been hard. Choniates goes on to say that the captives resettled at Philomelium were assigned land, given grain and seed, and granted tax immunity for five years—and that these terms were deemed so attractive that many other Byzantine subjects who had not been taken captive "preferred to settle among the barbarians rather than in the Hellenic cities and gladly quit their homelands" to join the deportees.[62]

Well before Kaykhusraw's final raid, Oğuz Turks had begun to migrate from their central Asian homelands to the Middle East, leading to the establishment of the first great Middle Eastern Turkish state, the Seljuk Empire, in the mid-11th century. The Seljuks soon came into conflict with their Byzantine neighbors; a notable episode in this conflict was the battle of Manzikert (Malazgirt) in eastern Anatolia in 1071, in which the Byzantine army was defeated and the emperor Romanos IV Diogenes captured by the forces of the Seljuk sultan Arp Aslan.

After Manzikert, the eastern Byzantine frontier collapsed, thanks to a combination of Seljuk pressure and internal dissension, paving the way for the mass movement of Turkish nomads (Turcomans) into Asia Minor and for the emergence of a powerful independent state, the Seljuk Sultanate of Rum, based in Iconium (Konya). By the time of Kaykhusraw's raid on Caria, the entire Anatolian plateau had come under Seljuk control. The upper Maeander valley, including the region around Aphrodisias, lay on the frontier between the Byzantine Empire and the Sultanate of Rum. Both Mangaphas's and Kaykhusraw's attacks should thus be understood as border conflicts in this contested frontier zone.

Half a century later, in AD 1243, the Sultanate of Rum succumbed to the Mongols, leading to further migration of Turks into western Asia Minor. While the Seljuk kingdom continued to exist as a Mongol vassal state, a new form of political organization appeared around its borders, in the form of independent principalities known as Beyliks, of which two of the most important were that of Menteşe, in the territory of ancient Caria, and that of the Osmanoğulları, or Ottomans, in northwestern Asia Minor. Eventually, of course, the Ottomans emerged as the most powerful of these states, and within two centuries of the Mongol defeat of the Seljuks, all of Anatolia except Constantinople and its territory had come under Ottoman domination.

In spite of Kaykhusraw's deportation of the population, Aphrodisias remained a Byzantine possession until the mid- or later 13th century. By 1278, however, according to the Byzantine historian George Pachymeres, "the region around the Maeander and Caria and Antioch had been lost."[63] It may initially have been under nominal Seljuk control, but by around 1365, it had apparently been incorporated into the Beylik of Menteşe.[64]

Both Menteşe and the neighboring Beylik of Aydın were conquered by the Ottomans in 1390, briefly restored to independence in 1402, and then finally reconquered by the Ottomans in 1424. The region around Aphrodisias lay on the border between Menteşe and Aydın, and it is possible that it had been transferred to the latter before the Ottoman conquest. By the date of the first Ottoman administrative records for the region in the mid-16th century, at any rate, it belonged to the province of Aydın, which remains the case to this day.

The brief discussion that follows of the history of Aphrodisias and the surrounding region in the Ottoman and modern Turkish (Republican) periods centers on four interlocking themes: the continued occupation of Aphrodisias itself, the emergence of Karacasu as the local market town and population center, the development of a network of rural villages and a regional road system, and the rediscovery of ancient Aphrodisias. The chapter will end with a brief examination of the current state of Aphrodisias and the surrounding region, and of the challenges and opportunities it faces in the future.

Ottoman and Modern Turkish Aphrodisias

The effect of Kaykhusraw's deportation of the inhabitants of Aphrodisias/ Caria at the very end of the 12th century is clearly legible in the archaeological record. There are no 13th-century Byzantine coins from the site and no objects after ca. 1200 from the excavated graves in the large cemetery east of the Cathedral. Study of the pottery from the excavations on the Theater hill and on the east side of the Agora has illuminated the subsequent habitation.[65] While fragments of imported 13th-century Byzantine and Seljuk pottery show that Aphrodisias was not completely or immediately abandoned, the absence of pottery datable to the 14th century suggests that for a few generations, occupation—presumably consisting of a combination of descendants of the original inhabitants and Turcoman nomads—was at best very limited. The 15th century witnessed the reappearance of a local tradition of pottery production, which continued until the 19th century. In addition to locally produced wares, imported pottery includes examples of the standard Ottoman export wares of the 15th to 19th centuries from İznik, Kütahya, and Çanakkale, as well as a small number of European imports, such as a single piece of late 18th- to early 19th-century Meissen porcelain.

The Ottoman village on the site of Aphrodisias is first mentioned by European travelers under the name of Geyre, presumably a corruption of Caria. It occupied the east central portion of the Roman city, extending northward from the two most ancient centers of habitation, the prehistoric Theater and Pekmez mounds, along the east side of the former Agora and Sanctuary of Aphrodite. Most of the village houses were removed in the course of archaeological excavation in the 1960s and 70s. The only remaining public buildings of note are two small bath complexes, one on the Pekmez hill, the other on the level ground to the north. The baths were apparently supplied by aqueducts bringing water from the northwest. Remnants of a terracotta pipeline supported by a bridge across the Derince Deresi (also known as the Geyre Çayı) approximately 1.5 km northwest of the site may belong to this aqueduct, as well as two stone towers just outside the northeast city wall of Aphrodisias (figs. 6.1–2). The latter are apparently *suterazi* towers, which served among other purposes to relieve pressure in buried pipelines, by bringing the water up to open tanks at the tops of the towers.

The village of Geyre was damaged in an earthquake in 1956. Rather than rebuilding on the long-since recognized ruins of Aphrodisias, the local authorities took this occasion to relocate the village to a new site 2 km to the west, as discussed in greater detail below.[66]

Karacasu

The earliest known Ottoman records of the region around Aphrodisias, dated to the year 1530, refer to the town (*kaza*) of Yenişehir as well as numerous dependent villages, of which several are recognizable from modern toponyms: Karacasu, Eymürlü, Gerye (*sic*), Sek, and Yazırlu.[67] Later records make it clear that Yenişehir was combined with Karacasu, the modern *ilçe*, or district capital, while Eymürlü is modern Ataeymir,

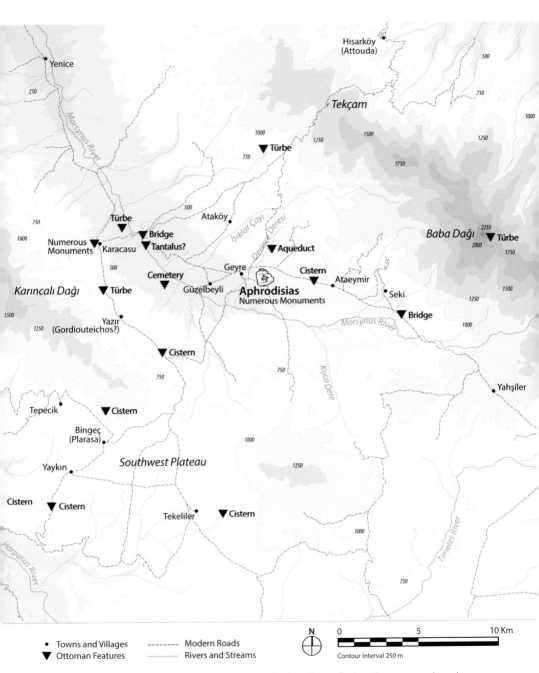

Fig. 6.1. Map of Aphrodisias survey region, showing locations of select Ottoman and modern Turkish points of interest.

Fig. 6.2. Possible pressure-regulating water tower (suterazi) at Aphrodisias.

Gerye modern Geyre, Sek modern Seki, and Yazırlu modern Yazır. Although Karacasu was not included in the Aphrodisias Regional Survey, its history may be summarized briefly here.

Karacasu lies at the west edge of the upper Morsynus River valley, at the base of Karıncalı Dağı (fig. 6.3). It overlooks a natural fork in the road coming eastward from the Maeander River valley, with one branch leading on the north side of the valley toward Tavas, the other leading on the south side of the valley toward the southwest plateau. This strategic location may be one of the reasons why it emerged as the major town in the region in the Ottoman era. Karacasu is spread over the east and west sides of a streambed known as the Tabakhane Deresi: the section to the west is called Çarşıyaka, that to the east Karşıyaka.

Fig. 6.3. View toward Karacasu, with Karındere tumulus in foreground, looking west.

Fig. 6.4. Eighteenth-century inscription naming Karacasu over doorway of Hacı Arap mosque.

As noted above, Ottoman records show that Karacasu existed as early as 1530, when it seems to have been independent of but associated with the town (*kaza*) of Yenişehir. The oldest inscription in the town, built into a fountain in the courtyard of the Hacı Ali Ağa or Çarşı (Market) mosque (in Çarşıyaka), is dated to 1591–1592. The name Karacasu is locally attested in an inscription dated to 1748 on the Hacı Arap mosque (in Karşıyaka; fig. 6.4). According to one tradition, the name comes from that of a nomadic tribal clan that established a village on this location; alternatively, it may come from the waters of the Tabakhane Deresi (Karacasu coming from *kara su*, or "dark water"). In either case, it is possible that Karacasu was the original name of the village on or near the site of Yenişehir—and perhaps always the name by which the town was known locally. It replaced Yenişehir as the official name of the town in the late 19th century. Karacasu was incorporated as a *kaza* in the province of Aydın in 1867, and as an *ilçe* in the same province in 1923.

By the mid-19th century, the town of Karacasu had a population of approximately 6,500 inhabitants, and that figure has remained remarkably constant for the last century and a half. In 2010, the population of the town was 6,108, and that of the entire *ilçe*, or administrative district, was 20,389.[68]

Fig 6.5. Ottoman bridge over Morsynus (Dandalas) River, before damage in 2015.

Among the historic buildings in the town in addition to the mosques mentioned above, special interest attaches in light of the road network discussed below to a bridge crossing from Çarşıyaka to Karşıyaka, known as the Karşıyaka bridge and dated to 1754. Unfortunately, its earlier fabric has now been completely obscured by modern construction. A second Ottoman bridge crosses the Morsynus River just east of Karacasu, near the confluence of the Tabakhane Deresi and the Morsynus, now known as the Dandalas (figs. 6.1, 6.5). Undated, it may be contemporary with the Karşıyaka bridge. The Dandalas bridge was sadly damaged during restoration efforts in 2015.[69]

Rural Villages and Roads

Of the villages listed in the 16th-century Ottoman record cited above in the region of Karacasu that have retained their early modern names, Ataeymir and Yazır remain among the most important local communities. Ataeymir is the largest village in the district besides Karacasu, with a population of 1,441, while Yazır is the largest village on the south side of the upper Morsynus River valley, with a population of 528. Both villages are located on important roads: Ataeymir on the main road leading from Karacasu to Tavas, and Yazır on the road leading from Karacasu to

Fig. 6.6. Ottoman cistern on southwest plateau near Tepecik.

the southwest plateau. Archaeologically, the most striking remains of the Ottoman regional road system are bridges and cisterns.

One road led up along the Morsynus River from the Maeander valley to the plain of Tabae, more or less along the line of the modern highway (substantial portions of the early road are preserved south of the modern road west of Güzelbeyli). Remains in the Morsynus valley include a masonry bridge at modern Esençay (southwest of Karacasu), the Dandalas bridge mentioned above near the confluence of the Tabakhane Deresi and the Morsynus, a cistern between the modern villages of Geyre and Ataeymir, and a bridge near the village of Seki, which is actually a Roman aqueduct bridge widened so as to carry wheeled traffic (see figs. 6.1, 3.30–31).

A second road attested by a single ruined cistern east of Yazır apparently led from Karacasu via Yazır to the southwest plateau. Like the road described above, it too follows the same line as the modern road. A third road also attested by a single cistern near the village of Tepecik probably ran from Bingeç westward along the south side of the Karıncalı Dağı (figs. 6.1, 6.6). Of great interest is a fourth road, which ran along the south side of the southwest plateau, attested by two cisterns around 3 km apart southwest of the village of Yaykın, and a third cistern approximately 8 km farther east near the village of Tekeliler (see fig. 6.1). According to the plausible

Fig. 6.7. Inscription over doorway of Ottoman cistern near Tekeliler.

Fig. 6.8. Ottoman cemetery by South
Necropolis outside Aphrodisias.

account of one local informant, these cisterns marked the line of a road
leading from Bozdoğan in the valley of the Harpasus River to Tavas on
the plain of Tabae. The cistern near Tekeliler bears an inscription over the
doorway with a date of 1216, or AD 1854/55, along with a modern inscription dating to AD 1964 (fig. 6.7).

The three cisterns of this last group are more or less uniform in size,
with diameters of 10–10.5 m. They consist of cylindrical drums constructed
of mortared subashlar or rubble masonry 2.25–2.65 m high, surmounted
by low domes. All have arched doorways. The most elaborate of the six
recorded cisterns, such as those near Tekeliler and Ataeymir, each have an
interior stairway leading down from the doorway to the floor of the cistern.
Some are also lit by two windows in addition to the doorway. The ruined
cistern near Yazır is similar in size, while the much better-preserved example near Tepecik is similar to the cistern at Tekeliler but slightly smaller

Fig. 6.9. Ottoman cemetery with schist grave markers on high ridge connecting Baba Dağı to Tekçam, looking north.

(8.6 m in diameter). The cistern between Geyre and Ataeymir is different in that it forms a 19-sided polygon in outline (see fig. 7.12). Although all of these cisterns are now derelict, their heritage persists in that the roads they marked remain for the most part in use.

Apart from modern villages, the main forms of evidence for Ottoman occupation of the landscape knit together by these roads are rural cemeteries and tombs. Notable cemeteries recorded by the Aphrodisias Regional Survey are found between Yazır and Güzelbeyli, perhaps associated with the village of Yazır noted in Ottoman records and including one headstone with a date of 1856; in the South Necropolis outside Aphrodisias, where there is also a modern *türbe*, or tomb monument, of a local religious figure (discussed below); and high up on the ridge between Baba Dağı and Tekçam, where the burials are marked with uninscribed schist slabs (figs. 6.1, 6.8–9). The *ilçe* of Karacasu contains a number of locally celebrated *türbeler* (tombs of holy men), of which the most famous is that of Dedebağ Dedesi—now the site of an important annual festival—on the outskirts of the Karacasu Yaylası south of Karacasu. Others include Süleyman Rüştü *türbesi* in the center of Karacasu, Yarem Dede *türbesi* southwest of Karacasu, and Şeyh Kemal *türbesi*, 5 km northeast of Ataköy. Two simple *türbeler* are situated on the outskirts of Aphrodisias, one just outside the Southeast Gate, the other just outside the South Gate; the

Fig. 6.10. Stone enclosure said to mark tomb of Baba Dağı Dedesi.

former is known as the tomb of Yukarı Dede (Upper Grandfather), the latter as Aşağı Dede (Lower Grandfather). Other rustic *türbeler* are found throughout the countryside, most dramatically a stone enclosure said to mark the tomb of Baba Dağı Dedesi, just east of the summit of Baba Dağı (fig. 6.10).

The Rediscovery of Aphrodisias

The first European traveler to visit Aphrodisias, describe the ruins, and record the texts of inscriptions was the British consul at Smyrna, William Sherard, in 1705.[70] Just over a century later, in 1812, the architect J. P. Gandy-Deering visited on behalf of the Society of the Dilletanti; his drawings were later published in *Antiquities of Ionia*, vol. III (1840). In the early 20th century, the first substantial excavations at the site were carried out under the direction of P. Gaudin (1904–5), and a second expedition was undertaken by an Italian team in 1937–38. As noted above, the Ottoman village of Geyre, situated in the northeast corner of Aphrodisias, was damaged in an earthquake in 1956, and the local authorities, long cognizant of the site's archaeological heritage, subsequently decided to relocate the population to a new site 1 km west of the west City Wall (in retrospect, it would have been even wiser to build the new village still farther away, for it rests on top of one of the cemeteries of the ancient city). As a planned settlement near the center of the Morsynus River valley, New Geyre attracted new settlers from a number of the valley's more remote villages in addition to the population of Old Geyre (see fig. 3.8). Its population at the census

Fig. 6.11. Wheat fields in Morsynus River valley, looking west.

of 2010 was 956. In 1961, shortly after the construction of the new village began, new excavations at Aphrodisias were launched by Kenan Erim of New York University. By the 1980s, the relocation of the village population was complete; all but a handful of the old village houses had been demolished; many of the civic and sacred buildings of the center of the city had been revealed, with remarkable finds of marble sculpture; an archaeological museum had been built on the site; and the entire area within the City Wall had been declared a protected archaeological zone. Erim died in 1990, and since then work has continued under the overall direction of R. R. R. Smith, focusing on continued study of the civic and sacred architecture, and on study and publication of sculpture. Aphrodisias is now a significant tourist destination, visited by tens of thousands of foreign and domestic tourists annually (over the past two decades, the numbers have fluctuated from a high of ca. 215,000 in 1997 to a low of ca. 80,000 in 1999; in 2010, the number of visitors was ca. 140,000).[71]

The Future of the Region around Aphrodisias

Aphrodisias lies in a rural region, largely dominated by agriculture. Crops under cultivation today throughout the surrounding area (the *ilçe* of Karacasu) include cereals (40 percent of the area under cultivation), tobacco (18 percent, obviously not grown in antiquity and now being replaced by olive), olive (14 percent and increasing), legumes (9 percent), vegetables (7 percent), apple (2 percent), fig (2 percent), and grape (just under 1 percent) (fig. 6.11).[72] Other local industries include pottery, for which Karacasu is locally

Fig. 6.12. A hiker on Baba Dağı, looking northwest.

famous, weaving (although the local textile industry has been severely undercut by Chinese imports), and marble quarrying (see figs. 1.7–8).

Tourism centers around Aphrodisias and has much to contribute to the local community. Aphrodisias itself is well protected, but the same cannot be said about the archaeological heritage of the surrounding countryside. In addition to its academic goals, the Aphrodisias Regional Survey was also very concerned with the conservation of the entire region. Loosely regulated marble quarrying threatens both the pastoral beauty of the upper Dandalas River valley and its ancient monuments, and casual looting is widespread. By documenting regional archaeological monuments, and by meeting and sharing our data and maps with local administrative, educational, and security officials, we hoped to heighten awareness and respect for the area's priceless archaeological heritage.

One additional way to improve the protection of these rural monuments would be through combined development of the ecological as well as the cultural resources of the region. The local landscape is one of great natural beauty, dominated by the majestic peak of Baba Dağı, which offers splendid opportunities for walking and hiking (fig. 6.12). Other natural attractions include the Morsynus River itself, especially the gorge east of Karacasu; a 450-m-deep cave on the south side of the Morsynus River valley (Sırtlanini) (fig. 6.13); and the dramatic canyons near the village of Yukarı Görle on the south side of the southwest plateau (fig. 6.14). The rural villages throughout the valley are also places of considerable rustic charm; especially beautiful is the Karacasu Yaylası, a small settlement in

Fig. 6.13. Survey team inside cave (Sırtlanini Mağarası) on south side of Morsynus River valley.

Fig. 6.14. Karabağlar canyon, near village of Yukarı Görle on south side of southwest plateau (photograph courtesy of Aydın Kültür ve Turizm İl Müdürlüğü, Türkiye, and Kanyon ve Doğa Sporları Araştırma Derneği, İstanbul).

Fig. 6.15. Tea
garden at
Karacasu Yaylası
(photograph
by Armağan
Portakal).

the wooded upland hills south of Karacasu, which offers cool evening breezes even in the hottest summer months (fig. 6.15). The final section of this book offers a sample half-day automobile tour of the region around Aphrodisias, with suggestions for further driving and hiking excursions at appropriate points.

7 A TOUR OF THE COUNTRYSIDE OF APHRODISIAS

The following driving tour takes the traveler from Aphrodisias westward to Karacasu, then southward out of the Morsynus valley to the adjoining plateau, continuing northeastward around Avdan Dağı to the Yahşiler pass, then returning northwestward to Aphrodisias (fig. 7.1). The tour covers a distance of 90 km and takes several hours or more, depending on the number of stops one makes. It is a pleasant journey, beginning in lush farmlands, climbing through forested slopes to an austere but dramatic tableland, winding alongside deep gorges, and ending with a descent through cool and sweetly pine-scented mountain air back into the valley. Hiking enthusiasts can also follow the recommended routes up to the summit of Baba Dağı. All along the journey are reminders of the past—not always immediately apparent but never hard to find. The purpose of this book has been to help the reader understand how the people who came before us interacted with this landscape. We hope the reader will use this tour as a launching pad for further exploration—either on the ground, by visiting these sites in person, or from the comfort of home, in a journey of the imagination.

Section 1

The tour begins at the turnoff to Aphrodisias from the main east–west road running through the Morsynus River valley. The site of Aphrodisias is located to the southwest, about 500 m down the road from the turnoff. Instead of turning off to the site, the traveler should turn in the opposite direction, heading northeast on the road leading through the hamlet of Dörtyol to the village of Palamutçuk, 4.5 km northeast of Aphrodisias. Just 1.5 km along the way, this road passes by an extensive series of ancient marble quarries; the quarry faces and the spoil heaps in front of them are clearly visible. On the right (east) side of the road is a modern quarry—the only large modern quarry on the north side of the valley. Palamutçuk lies

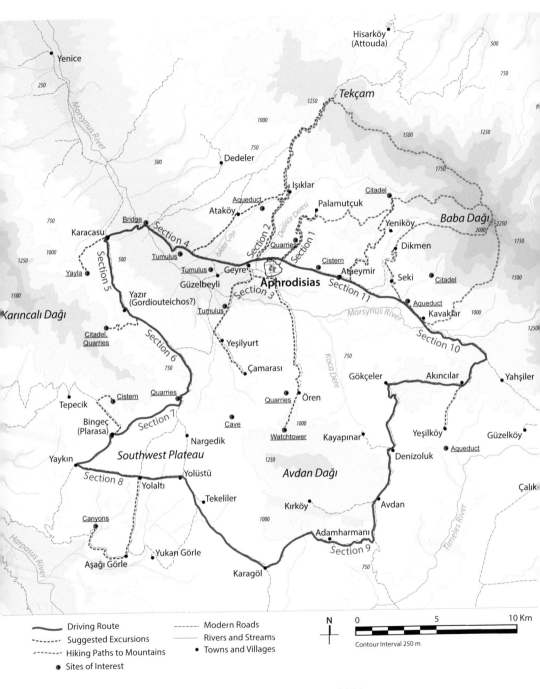

Fig. 7.1. Map of Aphrodisias survey region, showing route of driving tour.

hidden in the hills behind the quarries. A tractor path leading eastward from the village eventually joins up with one of the ridges climbing toward Baba Dağı; this is the most direct route from Aphrodisias to the mountain.

City Quarries. The marble quarries north of Aphrodisias are the largest series of ancient quarries in the Morsynus River valley and extend over an area of ca. 1 km² on the north and west slopes of a series of three hills (see pp. 64–65). To get to the largest quarry, with its 20-m-high pickmarked quarry face, head up the road to Palamutçuk for 1.5 km (about two-thirds of the way to the modern quarry), then park your car. The quarries lie on the west (far) slope of the hill to your left (west) at a distance of about 5 minutes' walk across the fields.

Path to Baba Dağı (fig. 7.2). The hike to the summit of Baba Dağı is long (35 km round trip from Aphrodisias and back) and strenuous (with an elevation gain of 1,800 m), but the rewards are high ridge walks and panoramic views. You begin at the turnoff to Aphrodisias on the main east–west road through the valley. Walk 4.5 km up the paved road to Palamutçuk, then turn right (east) up an unpaved tractor path just before entering the village. This leads to a small upland plateau, with a pond in the middle and a cluster of houses on the slopes on the east side. Continue eastward past the houses, toward the ridge leading up to the mountain. Eventually the path will join up with another tractor road leading northward from the village of Yeniköy, and it will take you right past a substantial ancient citadel at an elevation of 1250 m (see pp. 35–38). From here, the path leads due east along the north side of the ridge, and then eventually to the top of the ridge, where it disappears—but from this point the way forward to the summit is obvious. You can see the high ridge leading southeast from Tekçam to Baba Dağı clearly; it is marked by occasional tall cairns. Head for the cairns, and then follow the high ridge toward the mountain. The only really difficult part of the hike comes just before the summit of the mountain. The ridge leading to the mountain terminates in a steep cliff (fig. 7.3). You must cross from left to right along the base of the cliff to a chute on the right-hand side. The climb up the chute is a bit of a scramble, requiring the use of both hands as well as feet, but it leads you quickly to the steep slope at the top of the mountain. Here there is a lot of loose stone, but the final climb to the summit is straightforward. The summit itself is marked by a pair of tall cairns, and it offers grand views back to the southwest over the Morsynus River valley—the entire area covered by

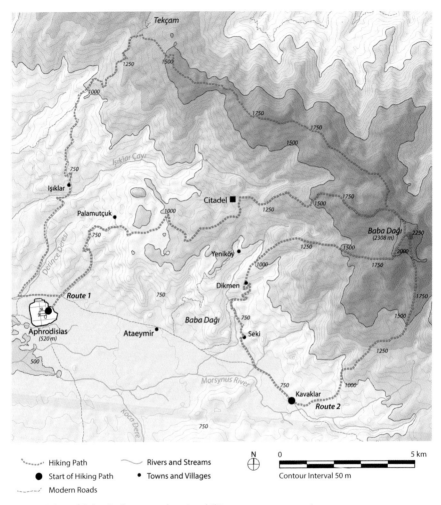

Fig. 7.2. Map of Baba Dağı range, showing hiking routes to summit.

the Aphrodisias Regional Survey is visible—and to the northeast and north-west to the Maeander and Lycus River valleys. The white cliffs of Pamukkale, ancient Hierapolis, may be clearly seen to the northeast. Either return to Aphrodisias the way you came, or, for a longer walk, go back to the cairns on the ridge to the northwest, and then, instead of turning to the west, continue along the top of the high ridge. Eventually you will come across a tractor path that leads all the way to the pass between the Morsynus and Maeander

Fig. 7.3. Summit of Baba Dağı, showing route of final ascent, looking southeast.

valleys at Tekçam (discussed below; the distance from the peak to the pass is 14 km). From Tekçam, you then walk along the road leading southwest back down into the Morsynus valley. Take the left-hand turn to Işıklar, then follow the road through Işıklar, and back to the main east–west road to Aphrodisias. The total length of the longer walk is 54 km; it took two experienced hikers 16 hours to complete it in 2016.

Section 2

Returning to the turnoff and then continuing westward along the main east–west road (with the site of Aphrodisias to the left [south]), the traveler reaches another crossroads after 1.5 km. The right-hand turn leads northeast to the village of Işıklar. It passes through a substantial cemetery of rock-cut tombs on the west (right) bank of a seasonal stream, crosses the stream, climbs a hill (with a modern cemetery on the right at the top of the hill), and then descends to Işıklar. After passing through the village, the traveler has two options. The first is to continue to the right along a road that leads up to the only pass connecting the valley of the Morsynus with the plain at the confluence of the Lycus and the Maeander Rivers to the north. The modern name of the pass is Tekçam, or Lone Pine, so called after a grand old tree at the top of the pass. From Tekçam, there is a tractor path that runs along the ridge climbing up to Baba Dağı (as noted above), and this provides another long (14 km) but relatively easy path to the mountain (except for the final ascent, discussed above). Alternatively, the traveler can take the left-hand turn from Işıklar, which leads to the village of Ataköy (4 km along the road). This road goes along the north (right) bank of a seasonal stream, and approximately 1.5 km from Işıklar it passes by the remains of a Roman aqueduct bridge on the opposite side of the stream. After visiting the aqueduct, the traveler can then either retrace his or her steps through Işıklar or continue along the road to and through Ataköy (in the hills above which there is a small cluster of ancient settlements) and back to the main east–west road, a few kilometers west of the turnoff to Işıklar.

> **Işıklar aqueduct bridge.** Only one pier of the Işıklar aqueduct bridge survives (see pp. 72–73). It is visible from the road down a steep slope to the left (south) of the road 1.5 km from the turnoff outside Işıklar.

Section 3

Opposite the turnoff to Işıklar is one of the roads leading to the modern village of Geyre; the main entrance to the village is on the left (south), 400 m farther down the road. As noted elsewhere, the village was established in the 1960s. Its predecessor, which occupied part of the ancient site, had been partially destroyed in an earthquake, and the authorities, recognizing the value of the archaeological remains at Aphrodisias, decided to rebuild the village on a new site 1 km outside the city walls. In the farming season, the fields that stretch out in every direction are hubs of quiet activity. Signs of the past are also omnipresent, in the ancient blocks seen frequently in modern field walls, in the scattered potsherds underfoot, and especially in the places where modern plowing has churned up piles of ancient bricks and roof tiles.

Fig. 7.4. Yeşilyurt tumulus, looking southwest.

Two roads lead out of Geyre to the south. One unpaved road leads to the southwest, crossing the Morsynus River at a ford manageable throughout most of the year except in springtime; as it begins to climb the hills on the south side of the valley, it passes a small tumulus tomb on the right (west), approximately 3.5 km from Geyre. It then continues through the village of Yeşilyurt and eventually terminates at the village of Çamarası. This provides the best access to the cave of Sırtlanini. The other road, which is paved, heads off to the southeast, crossing the river on a modern bridge and then climbing up the south side of the valley to the village of Ören. Ören means ruin, and the village may take its name from a poorly preserved watchtower on the hilltop just 1 km to the north; a much better-preserved watchtower lies 2 km south of the village.[73] To the west is a modern marble quarry, apparently also worked in antiquity.

Yeşilyurt tumulus. The unpaved road leading from modern Geyre to the villages of Yeşilyurt and Çamarası crosses the Morsynus River 3 km southwest of Aphrodisias. A distance of 0.7 km farther along, as the road begins to climb the still gentle slopes of the south side of the valley, it passes a small tumulus tomb about 100 m west of the road (fig. 7.4; see also pp. 27–28). The tumulus was cleaned out by the Aphrodisias Museum in 1982. It is still accessible, although it has partially filled in with loose earth. The chamber complex consists of a chamber, antechamber, and dromos (entrance corridor),

Fig. 7.5. Ancient and modern marble quarry workings near Ören.

oriented east–west with the entrance facing east. It is built out of fine lime-stone masonry, with partially preserved schist slabs that once carried the bodies of the deceased projecting from the back and south (left) walls of the chamber.

Çamarası cave. The Sırtlanini Mağarası (Hyena Cave) lies about 1.5 km south of Çamarası at an elevation of 1,060 masl (see fig. 6.13). The best way to get to the cave is to drive to Çamarası and ask for a guide. The cave is 450 m long and has a maximum depth below the entrance level of 40 m.

Ören watchtowers and quarries. The northern watchtower lies on the top of the hill on the east side of the road 1 km north of the village. To get to the better-preserved southern watchtower, take the road heading south out of the village, then bear left at the fork just south of the village. Follow the dirt road for another 1.9 km. The watchtower lies on the crown of the ridge to the east, in the maquis on the south side of a large field (see pp. 33–35). The modern and ancient marble quarries are located ca. 0.5 km west of the village of Ören, from which they are clearly visible (fig. 7.5).

Section 4

Returning to Geyre and continuing to the west, the main east–west road passes turnoffs to the south (left) to the village of Güzelbeyli, and then to the right (north) to Ataköy. Visible to the left between the road and Güzelbeyli is a large unexcavated tumulus. Continuing westward, the road crosses two deep gullies. Just before the second (western) gully is another tumulus tomb on the left (south) side of the road, now overlooking the Karacasu town dump. The road then descends gradually to the floor of the valley. Visible to the left (south) on the opposite side of the river is a distinctive flat-topped hill, crowned by the remains of a Byzantine citadel (see p. 19). This is probably Medieval Tantalus, after which the river takes its modern name of Dandalas. Just before it reaches the river, the road forks. The right (north) fork continues northwest along the river; the ancient road to the Maeander valley probably followed this line. The left fork crosses the river and turns southwest toward Karacasu. The modern concrete bridge at the crossing was built in the 1950s to replace a still standing Ottoman bridge. Just before (north of) the bridges is a bountiful spring, used nowadays to supply a trout farm and until recently to operate a mill on the northeast (right) bank of the river. This is one of the most beautiful places in the valley (see fig. 1.6), now sadly spoiled by a tannery just across the river from the old mill.

Güzelbeyli tumulus. The tumulus is the largest of the tumuli in the survey region, ca. 10 m high and ca. 45 m in diameter (see p. 25). A trench dug down from the top of the mound was abandoned without success, and the tomb chamber remains undiscovered.

Karındere tumulus. Crowning the brow of a hill overlooking the Karındere, a tributary of the Morsynus, the tumulus is a prominent landmark (see fig. 6.3). Approximately 40 m in diameter, it contains an elaborate rock-cut chamber complex, carved out of the native limestone near the center of the mound.

Dandalas bridge. The Ottoman bridge crosses the river in a single span (see p. 128). The arch itself is built of mortared ashlar masonry, with the "spandrels" between the arch proper and the roadway on top of mortared rubble. As already noted, the bridge was damaged during reconstruction efforts in 2015.

Section 5

Continue on the left fork to the central square of Karacasu, passing the Ethnographic Museum next to the bus station just below the square. The square lies at the intersection of İstiklal Caddesi (running east–west) and Mustafa Kemal Paşa Caddesi (running north–south). The Hacı Ali Ağa Camii, a 16th-century building (certainly worth a visit), lies at the southwest corner of the intersection. If you continue straight (west) on İstiklal Caddesi, after 3.4 km you will reach the Karacasu Yaylası, a delightful place for a kebap lunch or a glass of tea (see fig. 6.15). To continue the tour, return to the central square of Karacasu, and turn to the south on Mustafa Kemal Paşa Caddesi in the direction of the plateau southwest of Aphrodisias. On the way out of town, the road crosses the eastern one of two deep gorges that run on either side of Karacasu; visible in the scarp of the gorge (as in many other places in the valley) is the dark red soil used in the pottery for which Karacasu is locally famous. The pottery district lies just across the bridge (see fig. 1.7).

Farther on, the road clings to the southwest side of the valley. The slopes to the southwest are forested; the more level area to the northeast is partially forested, partially under cultivation. Four km from Karacasu, the road passes by the village of Yazır. Directly above the village is an ancient citadel whose modern name is Gâvur Pazaryeri, or Marketplace of the Infidel. Ancient and modern marble quarries are located on the hillslopes below the citadel. Southeast of Yazır, farmlands extend all the way to the Morsynus River.

> **Karacasu Ethnographic Museum.** The museum contains a number of early Ottoman tombstones and inscriptions, as well as displays of weapons, household objects, and traditional costumes.

> **Yazır citadel and quarry.** To get to the citadel above Yazır, drive 0.9 km past the village to the turnoff to the right (south) for the Demirağlar marble quarries. Drive up the (very dusty) dirt road for 2.75 km past two big switchbacks until you pass a turnoff to the right, just before a modern quarry face. The turnoff leads after 0.5 km to the top of a ridge overlooking the village and the valley below. Park your car at the level area on the crown of the ridge.

Directly in front of you is a substantial quarry pit, with a sizeable spoil heap on one side. The citadel of Yazır lies on the top of the ridge to the northeast (in the direction of the valley; see pp. 31–33). The largest quarry, with a dramatic 33-m-high quarry face, lies on the opposite side of the ridge to the north-northeast (see pp. 66–69). You will reach it by cutting diagonally to the right across the slope of the ridge after about a five-minute walk. This quarry was the source of the mottled blue-gray marble widely used at Aphrodisias in the Roman period (especially for monolithic columns).

Section 6

Just after Yazır, the road enters pine forests from which it does not emerge until it has breached the plateau to the south. Approximately 4 km past Yazır, the road is intersected by a branch road that leads eastward for 2 km and then turns sharply to the north for another 1.5 km, at which point it reaches a junction with two other roads. The road branching off to the left leads northward to Güzelbeyli on the other side of the Morsynus River. The road continuing in the middle travels northeastward to modern Geyre. To the right, a third road leads southeastward to the villages of Yeşilyurt and Çamarası. (This is the same branch road used to access the Yeşilyurt tumulus and Çamarası cave from Geyre, described above in section 3.) The slopes south of Çamarası, extending eastward all the way to Ören, are strikingly barren and are now quarried widely for both marble and emery (figs. 7.6–7). After the intersection with the road to the east, the main road from Karacasu continues to the southeast and south. Shortly before it climbs up onto the southwest plateau, it passes by a place called Hançam, where there is a series of large modern and ancient marble quarries on the west side of the road.

> **Hançam quarries.** The ancient and modern marble quarries climb up the hill on the right (west) side of the road (see p. 65). The five surviving ancient quarries (three medium-sized [5 m high] and two small [0.5–2.5 m high]) are located on the lower slopes. Their pickmarked quarry faces are clearly visible (see fig. 3.24). The top of the hill has been extensively worked in recent times, removing any trace of possible earlier quarrying.

Fig. 7.6. Ancient
marble quarry
near Çamarası.

Fig. 7.6. Ancient
marble quarry
near Çamarası.

Fig. 7.7. Modern
emery quarry
near Çamarası.

Section 7

Continuing 1 km southward from Hançam, the edge of the southwest plateau is reached at 850 masl, approximately 15 km from Karacasu. The plateau is a broad, level, and largely treeless area and a place of grand vistas—of the peaks of Baba Dağı to the northeast, of the plain of Tabae and behind it Mount Salbake to the southeast, and of Madran Dağı to the west (see fig. 1.9). The region is intensively cultivated today, and a striking feature of the landscape is the prevalence of a dark red soil also found in places in the Morsynus valley.

Shortly after it emerges onto the plateau, there is a fork in the road. The right (west) fork branches off to the southwest to the villages of Bingeç and Yaykın. At Bingeç, a branch road diverges to the northwest, to the village of Tepecik. Tepecik lies at the foot of Karıncalı Dağı, and the slopes to the east and north of the village are dotted with modern marble quarries, rising all the way up to the crown of the ridge. East of Tepecik, a gravel road leads down past an Ottoman cistern into the valley of the Harpasus. Bingeç itself is the best-known archaeological site on the southwest plateau; a number of inscriptions built into modern walls were recorded by travelers beginning in the 19th century, and an extensive tumulus cemetery is situated just north of the village. As previously discussed, it has long been identified, probably correctly, as Plarasa, Hellenistic Aphrodisias's "sister city."

> **Tepecik cistern.** This cistern is located 2.2 km north of Bingeç, and 2.8 km southeast of Tepecik (see pp. 129–30). It is a circular structure, typical of Ottoman cisterns, consisting of a cylindrical drum, 8.6 m in diameter, surmounted by a slightly less than hemispherical dome. The walls of the drum are faced with small stone blocks; the rubble masonry of the dome is exposed; in other cisterns it is faced with lime mortar or cement. An arched doorway provides access and illumination to the interior of the cistern.

> **Bingeç.** Ancient architectural blocks are found throughout the walls and gardens of the village (although some of the inscriptions have recently been moved to the Aphrodisias Museum) (see fig. 4.10). The tumulus cemetery lies on a ridge 0.5 km north of Bingeç and is best reached with the aid of a local guide. All the actual tomb chambers are rock-cut, but in a few cases, surviving circular stone walls show that they were surmounted by earthen mounds or tumuli (fig. 7.8). A total of approximately 30 tombs are known.

Section 8

After visiting Bingeç, continue southwestward for 3 km toward Yaykın, then turn right on a branch road leading eastward to the villages of Yolaltı

Fig. 7.8. Remains of "crepis" wall of tumulus tomb at Bingeç, looking north.

Fig. 7.9. Survey team walking across saddle between Avdan Dağı and southern foothills of Baba Dağı, looking southwest.

and Yolüstü. At Yolaltı (4 km from Yaykın) in addition to continuing toward Yolüstü, a turnoff to the south leads to the villages of Aşağı Görle and Yukarı Görle, 30 km from Karacasu. These small settlements lie toward the south edge of the plateau and are hedged in by high cliffs. Carved into the cliffs are numerous rock-cut tombs. From Aşağı Görle, an extremely circuitous road leads to the valley of the Harpasus.

> **Görle canyons.** Near Görle are a series of dramatic natural canyons leading from the southwest plateau to the Harpasus River valley to the south. Most spectacular is the Karabağlar canyon, which lies between Aşağı Görle and the neighboring village of Karabağlar to the northwest (see fig. 6.14). The canyon is 2.5 km long, with a total elevation drop of 200 m, and features three dramatic waterfalls.[74] It is best reached with the aid of a local guide.

Section 9

Returning to Yolaltı, continue 2.75 km to Yolüstü, and then (just past the village) turn right (south) and continue to Tekeliler (2 km south of Yolüstü). From Tekeliler, a branch road runs southwestward to Görle, while the main road continues to the southeast around the south and east sides of Avdan Dağı, to the villages of Karagöl, Adamharmanı, and Avdan—the last approximately 50 km from Karacasu (17 km from Tekeliler). Between Karagöl and Adamharmanı, a branch road runs northward to the village of Kırköy. Ancient spolia are found collected in the town squares or built into houses and other buildings in many of these villages, including Middle Byzantine architectural fragments in Nargedik (located farther west, in the center of the plateau) and Avdan (see pp. 118–19). The south and east sides of Avdan Dağı slope gradually down to the valley of the Timeles River. North of Avdan, there is a broad saddle running between Avdan Dağı and the southern foothills of Baba Dağı, and separating the Morsynus River valley to the northwest from the valley of the Timeles to the southeast (fig. 7.9).

Three km north of Avdan, the road that runs around Avdan Dağı reaches the village of Denizoluk, located at the southern edge of the saddle. A branch road leading to the west terminates at the village of Kayapınar, near the head of a gorge running northwestward toward Aphrodisias. The name of the gorge is Koca Dere, or Big Stream. In the Roman

Fig. 7.10. View from area of Denizoluk to Baba Dağı, looking north.

period, the aqueduct that brought water from the Timeles River to Aphrodisias ran down the right bank of this streambed. The saddle northeast of Kayapınar and Denizoluk is a pleasant place of rolling hills beneath the towering presence of Baba Dağı, previously hidden behind Avdan Dağı to the south and west but now once again the dominant feature of the landscape (fig. 7.10). East of the saddle, the ground falls away sharply in a series of pine-forested ravines approaching the Timeles River. The refreshing sound of water running through the riverbed and its tributaries, even in midsummer, gives the landscape a character very different from that of the surrounding regions. Across the river is the sharp-edged plain of Tabae (modern Tavas Ovası).

After Denizoluk, the main road runs northward to the village of Gökçeler (5 km from Denizoluk), then turns eastward across the hills toward the town of Yahşiler, which lies just across the pass connecting the upper Morsynus River valley with the plain of Tabae to the east. In a hollow just before the junction with the east–west road that runs through the Morsynus valley, at the hamlet of Akıncılar (4 km from Gökçeler), there is a turnoff to the south, which leads to the small village of Yeşilköy (2.7 km south of Akıncılar). The best-preserved remains of the Roman aqueduct lie just southeast of this village.

Timeles aqueduct. The remains of the aqueduct, which lie 0.5–1.5 km south-east of Yeşilköy, are best reached with the aid of a local guide. They include sections of bridges built to carry the water over gorges, tunnels dug to carry it through hills, and, in connection with the tunnels, shafts dug down from the ground level to aid initially in digging the tunnels and to serve later on as inspection shafts. Most impressive is the 17-m-high standing bridge crossing the Kırkım Deresi, 0.75 km southeast of the village (see pp. 76–77).

Section 10

Returning to Akıncılar and continuing to the northeast, the road joins up after 3 km with the main road leading from Karacasu to Tavas just above the Yahşiler pass. Turn left (northwest) back toward the Morsynus River valley. The road levels out after a steep descent 5 km after the junction at a place whose local name is Kavaklar, a peaceful grove of plane trees. On the right (north) side of the road nearby is a very important spring still used today, and on the left (south) side of the road, a small Ottoman mosque next to a modern restaurant. Another hike to the summit of Baba Dağı starts from this spot. A further 1.6 km after Kavaklar (0.3 km before [east of] the turnoff to the village of Seki), the road crosses a modern concrete bridge over a seasonal streambed. Just upstream from the modern bridge is a much older bridge, which is in fact a Roman aqueduct bridge, widened in the Ottoman period to carry wheeled traffic.

Path to Baba Dağı (see fig. 7.2). The 13 km hike from Kavaklar to the summit of Baba Dağı is an overland walk with no marked trail—so not for the inexperienced. That said, it offers a more gradual approach to the mountain than the route leading directly from Aphrodisias, and the ridge southeast of the mountain is very beautiful. From Kavaklar, head southeast more or less parallel with the main road until you encounter a seasonal streambed. Follow the streambed for a few hundred meters. To your left (north) you will see a modern gravel quarry, and then after that a large solar panel array. Between the streambed and the solar panel array (as of the time of writing in 2016) is a large fenced-in olive grove. As you skirt the lower (south) edge of the olive grove, you will see a pine forested ridge in front of you, across another seasonal streambed (a tributary of the first). Head for and then (turning to the northeast) climb through increasingly taller pine trees up this ridge. Once you have emerged from the tall pines (and the ground has leveled off a bit), bear to the right (on the east side of the ridge). Further to your right you will eventually see a clear-cut section of forest. Keeping this on your right (and crossing a gully), you will find yourself on another ridge. You can now follow this ridge straight up to the top of the mountain—or, for a more varied walk, continue to bear right, keeping the ridge on your left. At a certain point you will see yet another ridge in front of you, leading southeast–northwest all the way to the summit. Cross two more steep gorges, and then climb to the crown of this ridge. From this point onward (6 km from Kavaklar) the way is clear—you will climb up through a scattering of ancient juniper and pine trees, many blasted by the frequent lightning storms that sweep along the mountain range, until you reach a small depression below the final ascent to the mountain. Then it is straight up above the tree line to the ridge that runs along the top of the mountain (being careful to maintain a safe distance from the steep cliff to your right); the summit is at the northwest end of this ridge. Either return the way you came, or head down the ridge to the southwest, being careful not to lose your footing on the loose stone. After 1 km, turn right in the direction of a low peak about 1.5 km to the west. Skirting the south side of this peak, you will come to a steep east–west cliff (just north of the peak). Walk westward parallel with the edge of this cliff for about 1.5 km until you reach a dirt road, which you can then follow all the way into the village of Dikmen. From Dikmen, you can walk down the paved road through Seki (making sure to bear to the left) until you reach the main east–west road and then turn left and continue east back to Kavaklar. (Alternatively, you can arrange for a pickup in Dikmen, which cuts out the rather uninteresting walk along the paved road.)

Seki aqueduct bridge. The Roman aqueduct bridge, widened in the Ottoman period to carry wheeled traffic, lies just north (upstream) of the modern concrete bridge (see pp. 70–72). The original (Roman) part of the bridge is to the south (downstream), the Ottoman addition to the north (upstream).

Section 11

From the aqueduct bridge, continue westward toward the village of Seki. Just before (east of) the village, the road crosses the bed of another seasonal stream known as Kale Deresi, or Castle Stream, and there is indeed a fortified citadel towering over its east bank approximately 2 km upstream. The road then passes by turnoffs toward the villages of Seki, Dikmen, and Yeniköy, all located to the right (north) on the lower slopes of Baba Dağı, before reaching the prosperous village of Ataeymir (4.25 km from the Seki aqueduct bridge). There are signs of ancient settlement in the hills behind all three villages: north of Ataeymir, a walled village on a place called Asar Tepe, or Ruin Hill; in the highlands above Yeniköy, a Middle Byzantine church and a large walled citadel of much earlier date; and just north of Dikmen, a rock-cut tomb on the edge of a modern graveyard. In two places in Ataeymir itself, clusters of sarcophagi have been reused as modern fountains and watering troughs. According to the villagers, the sarcophagi were brought from Aphrodisias. Continuing westward from Ataeymir, the road passes by an Ottoman cistern after 1.5 km, before reaching the turnoff to Aphrodisias—the start and endpoint of our tour, 8 km from the Roman aqueduct bridge near Seki.

Seki citadel. The citadel is best reached with the aid of a local guide (see pp. 35–37).

Yeniköy citadel. Take the turnoff to Yeniköy on the right (north) just before (east of) Ataeymir. As it approaches the village, the road enters into a long switchback around the back of a gorge. Take the left-hand turn on a dirt road just before the switchback. Continue westward up this road until it intersects a north–south road, and turn right (north). Continue northward up this road for 2 km. For most of the way, the road is gradually climbing a ridge. At a certain point it reaches the top of the ridge and then descends sharply. Park your car at the base of this slope. The citadel lies on the hill (Oyukkıranı Tepesi) in front of you to the left (northwest) (see pp. 35–38).

Sarcophagi in Ataeymir fountains. A number of old village fountains in Ataeymir incorporate Roman sarcophagi allegedly brought from Aphrodisias. The best way to find them is to drive to the center of the village and ask for assistance. One such fountain combines a chain of ancient receptacles including

Fig. 7.11. Ancient sarcophagi and crushing basins reused in fountain in Ataeymir.

Fig. 7.12. Ottoman cistern on road between Ataeymir and Aphrodisias.

a garland sarcophagus, a crushing basin from an olive oil press, two more plain sarcophagi, and another crushing basin from an olive oil press (fig. 7.11).

Ataeymir cistern. This Ottoman cistern is different from the one mentioned above at Tepecik in that its lower part is polygonal (19-sided) rather than circular (fig. 7.12). It is also somewhat larger, with a diameter of 9.7 m. Like the Tepecik cistern, it is built of mortared rubble faced with subashlar masonry and surmounted by a low dome (in this case faced with concrete). Its doorway is located on the west side, and there is a narrow stairway carved out of a single block of marble leading from the threshold of the doorway to the floor of the cistern.

NOTES

1   *Aphrodisias V.*

2   Pliny, *Natural History* 5.108.

3   L. Robert and J. Robert, *La Carie* II (Paris 1954) 46–49.

4   Ibid., 43–46.

5   Livy, *History of Rome* 38.13.11.

6   *IAph2007* 2.506.

7   B. V. Head, *A Catalog of the Greek Coins in the British Museum, Caria, Cos, Rhodes, etc.* (London 1897) 101 with pl. 17.9.

8   Nicetas Choniates, *Historia,* ed. J.-L. van Dieten (Berlin 1975) 494–95.

9   For discussion, see ala2004 VII.27.

10 For full discussion, see J. Reynolds, "The Politeia of Plarasa and Aphrodisias," *Revue des études anciennes* 87 (1985) 213–18; A. Chaniotis, "New Evidence."

11 Joukowsky, *Prehistoric Aphrodisias*; eadem, "Prehistoric Developments on the Acropolis (Theater Hill)," *Aphrodisias Papers* 2, 9–13; A. Greaves, "Bronze Age Aphrodisias Revisited," in C. Gallou, M. Georgiadis, and G. M. Muskett (eds.), *Dioskouroi,* BAR-IS 1889 (Oxford 2008) 252–64.

12 This cave was explored in June 2007; the pottery was dated by Daniel Pullen (pers. comm.). An emery or micaschist axe head was found on the surface 2.5 km due south (and downhill) of the entrance to the cave. On the cave: Y. Aşkın, "Sırtlanini Mağarası," *Afrodisias Karacasu Tanıtım Dergisi* 3 (n.d.) 12–15; N. Güldalı, L. Nazik, C. Soylu, and B. Aksoy, *İzmir, Manisa, ve çevresinin doğal mağaraları,* MTA [Maden Tetkik ve Arama Enstitüsü] Raporu No. 7819 (Ankara 1985). Our thanks go to Dr. Oruç Baykara for his generous personal communications on the subject of his yet unpublished research.

13 J. de la Genière, "Premières recherches sur Aphrodisias préromaines," *Aphrodisias de Carie,* 53–64.

14 For a general treatment of Lydian and Carian interaction at Aphrodisias and elsewhere, see C. Ratté, "The Carians and the Lydians," in F. Rumscheid (ed.), *Die Karer und die Anderen* (Bonn 2009) 135–47.

15 F. Rumscheid, "Mylasas Verteidigung: Burgen statt Stadtmauer?" in E.-L. Schwandner and K. Rheidt (eds.), *Stadt und Umland* (Mainz 1999) 206–22.

16 Chaniotis, "New Evidence," 455–66.

17 For new evidence for this period, see A. Chaniotis and F. Rojas, "A Second Lydian Inscription from Aphrodisias," *Aphrodisias Papers* 5, 341–45.

18 C. Ratté, "The Founding of Aphrodisias," *Aphrodisias Papers* 4, 7–36.

19   Reynolds, *Aphrodisias and Rome*, 102–3; *IAph2007* 8.31.

20   C. Ratté, "The Urban Development of Aphrodisias in the Late Hellenistic and Early Imperial Periods," in C. Berns, H. von Hesberg, L. Vandeput, and M. Waelkens (eds.), *Patris und Imperium* (Leuven 2002) 5–32.

21   *Aphrodisias VI.*

22   K. Welch, "The Stadium at Aphrodisias," *American Journal of Archaeology* 102 (1998) 546–69.

23   This and the following figures were obtained from the Turkish Statistical Institute (Türkiye İstatik Kurumu). The authors are grateful to Burhanettin Korkmaz of the Data Dissemination Group for his assistance. The data are available electronically at: http://tuikapp.tuik.gov.tr/adnksdagitapp (accessed 11 August 2011).

24   W. Scheidel, "Demography," in W. Scheidel, I. Morris, and R. Saller (eds.), *The Cambridge Economic History of the Greco-Roman World* 1 (Cambridge 2007) 38–86, at 79, with references.

25   These figures are taken from the official Karacasu government website, which also lists numerous other agricultural products grown in the region today: www.karacasu.gov.tr/sg.asp? ID=258 (accessed 19 April 2009).

26   Roueché, *Performers and Partisans*, 168–73; Reynolds, *Aphrodisias and Rome,* 193–97; J. M. R. Cormack, "Epigraphic Evidence for the Water-Supply of Aphrodisias," *Annual of the British School at Athens* 49 (1954) 9–10.

27   Cato, *On Agriculture* 66.

28   H. Forbes and L. Foxhall, "'The Queen of All Trees': Preliminary Notes on the Archaeology of the Olive," *Expedition* 21.1 (1978) 37–47.

29   J.-P. Brun, *Archéologie du vin et de l'huile de la préhistoire à l'époque hellénistique* (Paris 2003) 7, 10.

30   Samples were taken from the Tetrapylon, Theater Baths, Tetrastoön, Gaudin's Gymnasium, Gaudin's Fountain, Hadrianic Baths, Tetrakionion, Triconch House, Atrium House, and the Temenos of the Temple of Aphrodite. For more on the isotopic signatures of the marbles in the survey region and at Aphrodisias, see C. Stearns, "Geoarchaeological Investigations," *Aphrodisias V*, 135–64.

31   R. R. R. Smith and C. H. Hallett, "Troilos and Achilles: A Monumental Statue Group from Aphrodisias," *Journal of Roman Studies* 105 (2015) 124–82.

32   J. Reynolds, "The Dedication of a Bath Building at Carian Aphrodisias," in A. Fol, B. Bogdanov, P. Dimitrov, and D. Boyadziev (eds.), *Studia in honorem Georgii Mihailov* (Sofia 1995) 397–402 (*IAph2007* 5.6); A. Wilson, "The Olympian (Hadrianic) Baths: Layout, Operation, and Financing," *Aphrodisias Papers* 5, 168–94. On the water-flow management system created during the reign of Domitian, see A. Chaniotis, "Twelve Buildings in Search of Locations: Known and Unknown Buildings in the Inscriptions," *Aphrodisias Papers* 4, 61–78. For recent research on water features within the city, see A. Wilson,

"Water, Nymphs, and a Palm Grove: Monumental Water Display at Aphrodisias," *Aphrodisias Papers* 5, 100–35.

33 Coins: F. Imhoof-Blumer, *Fluss-und Meergötter auf griechischen und römischen Münzen* (Geneva 1923) nos. 291, 292, pl. IX no. 28 (Aphrodisias); no. 295, pl. X no. 3 (Herakleia Salbakes). Construction of aqueduct: *IAph2007* 11.412; J. Reynolds, "New Letters from Hadrian to Aphrodisias: Trials, Taxes, Gladiators and an Aqueduct," *Journal of Roman Archaeology* 13 (2000) 5–20. "Introduction" of the Timeles River: *IAph2007* 12.1111; A.-V. Pont, "L'inscription en l'honneur de M. Ulpius Carminius Claudianus à Aphrodisias (CIG, 2782)," *Cahiers du Centre Glotz* 19 (2010) 219–45.

34 L. Robert and J. Robert, *La Carie* II (Paris 1954) 46–49.

35 Discharge estimates for the Aqua Claudia (184,220 m³ per day) and Anio Novus (189,520 m³ per day) come from A. T. Hodge, *Roman Aqueducts and Water Supply*, 2nd edition (London 2002) 347. For the revised estimate we thank Paul Kessener (pers. comm.).

36 *IAph2007* 12.909.

37 ala2004 IX.35–36, **165–66**.

38 P. D. De Staebler, "The City Wall and the Making of a Late Antique Provincial Capital," *Aphrodisias Papers* 4, 284–318.

39 F. Işık, *Girlanden-Sarkophage aus Aphrodisias* (Mainz 2007).

40 E. Öğüş, "Columnar Sarcophagi from Aphrodisias: Elite Emulation in the Greek East," *American Journal of Archaeology* 118 (2014) 113–36.

41 R. R. R. Smith, "Sarcophagi and Roman Citizenship," *Aphrodisias Papers* 4, 347–94.

42 On local martyrs at Aphrodisias, see ala2004 VII.23.

43 ala2004 V.18.

44 For the Syrian type, see G. Tchalenko, *Églises syriennes à Bêma* (Paris 1990); G. Tchalenko and E. Baccache, *Églises de village de la Syrie du Nord*, 2 vols. (Paris 1979–80); for examples in western Asia Minor, see U. Serin, *Early Christian and Byzantine Churches at Iasos in Caria: An Architectural Survey. Monumenti di antichità cristiana* II (Vatican City 2004) 173–76.

45 P. D. De Staebler, "The City Wall and the Making of a Late Antique Provincial Capital," *Aphrodisias Papers* 4, 284–318, at 297, 301–2.

46 ala2004 VII.23, **108**.

47 ala2004 IX.35, **166**.

48 P. D. De Staebler, "The City Wall and the Making of a Late Antique Provincial Capital," *Aphrodisias Papers* 4, 284–318, at 302.

49 A. Chaniotis, "Inscriptions," *Aphrodisias V*, 347–66, at 353–54, 365–66.

50 I. Lockey, "Olive Oil Production and Rural Settlement," *Aphrodisias V*, 203–37, at 225–26, using figures for oil yields in North Africa proposed by D. J. Mattingly, "The Olive Boom. Oil Surpluses, Wealth and Power in Roman Tripolitania," *Libyan Studies* 19 (1988) 21–41.

51   M. Berenfeld, "The Triconch House and the Predecessors of the Bishop's Palace at Aphrodisias," *American Journal of Archaeology* 113 (2009) 203–29, with references.

52   On the City Wall, see P. D. De Staebler, "The City Wall and the Making of a Late Antique Provincial Capital," *Aphrodisias Papers* 4, 284–318, at 297.

53   ala2004 VII.23, **108**.

54   P. D. De Staebler, "The City Wall and the Making of a Late Antique Provincial Capital," *Aphrodisias Papers* 4, 284–318, at 297.

55   H. Buchwald, "Retrofit—Hallmark of Byzantine Architecture?" in H. Buchwald, *Form, Style and Meaning in Byzantine Church Architecture* (Brookfield, VT 1999) 1–22, at 16–17.

56   See, for example, J. J. Coulton, *The Balboura Survey and Settlement in Highland Southwest Anatolia* (London 2012); H. Vanhaverbeke, A. K. Vionis, J. Poblome, and M. Waelkens, "What Happened after the 7th Century AD? A Different Perspective on Post-Roman Rural Anatolia," in T. Vorderstrasse and J. J. Roodenberg (eds.), *Archaeology of the Countryside in Medieval Anatolia* (Leiden 2009) 177–90; W. Anderson, "Settlement Change in Byzantine Galatia: An Assessment of Finds from the General Survey of Central Anatolia," *Anatolian Archaeological Studies: Kaman-Kalehöyük* 17 (2008) 233–40.

57   M. Dennert, "Mittelbyzantinische Ambone in Kleinasien," *Istanbuler Mitteilungen* 45 (1997) 137–47, at 138, pl. 49.1–2.

58   A. Zäh, *Zur Typologie kirchlicher Architektur im südwestlichen Kleinasien* (Maintal 2003) plan 2.0; R. M. Harrison, "Churches and Chapels of Central Lycia," *Anatolian Studies* 13 (1963) 117–51, at 130.

59   M. Panayotidi, "La peinture monumentale en Grèce de la fin de l'Iconoclasme jusqu'à l'avènement des Comnènes (843–1081)," *Cahiers archéologiques* 34 (1986) 75–108, at 75–83.

60   Nicetas Choniates, *Historia*, ed. J.-L. van Dieten (Berlin 1975) 494–95; see ala2004 VII.27–29 on the end of Byzantine Aphrodisias.

61   Ibid., 400; see ala2004 VII.9.

62   Nicetas Choniates, *Historia*, ed. J.-L. van Dieten (Berlin 1975) 494.

63   Georgius Pachymeres, *Relations historiques*, ed. A. Failler (Paris 1984) II, 591 (*Historia* 6.20).

64   P. Wittek, *Das Fürstentum Mentesche, Istanbuler Mitteilungen* 2 (Istanbul 1934) 166. Reference supplied by Gottfried Hagen.

65   V. François, "Éléments de l'histoire ottomane d'Aphrodisias: la vaisselle de terre," *Anatolia Antiqua* 9 (2001) 147–90.

66   For general discussion, see Erim, *Aphrodisias*, 18–19.

67   I. Binark and A. Özkılınç (eds.), *166 Numaralı Muhasebe-i Vilayet-i Anadolu Defteri (937/1530)* (Ankara 1995) 459-64. Warm thanks to Erdem Çıpa for his assistance with

this document. For the history of Karacasu, see http://www.karacasuaydin.bel.tr/Icer-ik.aspx?Id=62&Baslik=Karacasu%20İlçesi%20Tarihçesi (accessed 13 March 2016). For historic buildings in Karacasu, see *Aydın Kültür Envanteri* II (Ankara 2012) 151–57, 160–61, 163–64, 166–67, 175–89.

68   This and the following figures were obtained from the Turkish Statistical Institute (Türkiye İstatik Kurumu). We are grateful to Burhanettin Korkmaz of the Data Dissemination Group for his assistance. The data are available electronically at: http://tuikapp.tuik.gov.tr/adnksdagitapp (accessed 11 August 2011).

69   For a contemporary newspaper report, see http://www.hurriyet.com.tr/6-asirlik-dan-dalaz-koprusu-restorasyonda-yikildi-29970182.

70   On the history of early travelers to Aphrodisias, see *IAph2007*, "Bibliography."

71   M. Zekeriyal and P. Aykut, "The Importance of Aphrodisias Ancient City in Sustainable Economical Development," *3rd International Symposium on Sustainable Development* (Sarajevo 2102) 236–42.

72   www.karacasu.gov.tr/Karacasu.aspx?Sayfa_Ekonomi (accessed June 2006).

73   Ören has recently been aspirationally renamed Yeşilköy (Green Village).

74   http://www.aydinkulturturizm.gov.tr/TR,64618/karabaglar-kanyonu.html (accessed 14 July 2016).

BIBLIOGRAPHICAL ABBREVIATIONS

ala2004

C. Roueché, *Aphrodisias in Late Antiquity: The Late Roman and Byzantine Inscriptions*, revised 2nd edition (2004), http://insaph.kcl.ac.uk/ala2004.

Aphrodisias I

R. R. R. Smith, *Aphrodisias I. The Monument of C. Julius Zoilos* (Mainz 1993).

Aphrodisias II

R. R. R. Smith et al., *Aphrodisias II. Roman Portrait Sculpture from Aphrodisias* (Darmstadt/Mainz 2006).

Aphrodisias III

L. Brody, *Aphrodisias III. The Aphrodite of Aphrodisias* (Darmstadt/Mainz 2007).

Aphrodisias IV

P. Linant de Bellefonds, *Aphrodisias IV. The Mythological Reliefs from the Agora Gate* (Darmstadt/Mainz 2009).

Aphrodisias V

C. Ratté and P. D. De Staebler (eds.), *Aphrodisias V. The Aphrodisias Regional Survey* (Darmstadt/Mainz 2012).

Aphrodisias VI

R. R. R. Smith, *Aphrodisias VI. The Marble Reliefs from the Julio-Claudian Sebasteion at Aphrodisias* (Darmstadt/Mainz 2013).

Aphrodisias VII

P. Stinson, *Aphrodisias VII. The Civil Basilica* (Wiesbaden 2016).

Aphrodisias de Carie

J. de la Genière and K. T. Erim (eds.), *Aphrodisias de Carie* (Paris 1987).

Aphrodisias Papers 1

C. Roueché and K. T. Erim (eds.), *Aphrodisias Papers 1, Journal of Roman Archaeology*, Suppl. 1 (Ann Arbor 1990).

Aphrodisias Papers 2

R. R. R. Smith and K. T. Erim (eds.), *Aphrodisias Papers 2, Journal of Roman Archaeology*, Suppl. 2 (Ann Arbor 1991).

Aphrodisias Papers 3   R. R. R. Smith and C. Roueché (eds.), *Aphrodisias Papers* 3, *Journal of Roman Archaeology*, Suppl. 20 (Ann Arbor 1996).

Aphrodisias Papers 4   C. Ratté and R. R. R. Smith (eds.), *Aphrodisias Papers* 4, *Journal of Roman Archaeology*, Suppl. 70 (Portsmouth, RI 2008).

Aphrodisias Papers 5   R. R. R. Smith, J. Lenaghan, A. Sokolicek, and K. Welch (eds.), *Aphrodisias Papers* 5, *Journal of Roman Archaeology*, Suppl. 103 (Portsmouth, RI 2016).

Chaniotis, "New Evidence"   A. Chaniotis, "New Evidence from Aphrodisias Concerning the Rhodian Occupation of Karia and the Early History of Aphrodisias," in R. van Bremen and J.-M. Carbon (eds.), *Hellenistic Karia* (Bordeaux 2010) 455–66.

Chaniotis, "New Inscriptions"   A. Chaniotis, "New Inscriptions from Aphrodisias (1995-2001)," *American Journal of Archaeology* 108 (2004) 377–416.

Erim, *Aphrodisias*   K. T. Erim, *Aphrodisias: City of Venus Aphrodite* (London and New York 1986).

IAph2007   J. Reynolds, C. Roueché, and G. Bodard, *Inscriptions of Aphrodisias* (2007), http://insaph.kcl.ac.uk/iaph2007.

Joukowsky, *Prehistoric Aphrodisias*   M. S. Joukowsky, *Prehistoric Aphrodisias. An Account of the Excavations and Artifact Studies* (Louvain 1986).

Reynolds, *Aphrodisias and Rome*   J. M. Reynolds, *Aphrodisias and Rome, Journal of Roman Studies*, Monograph 1 (London 1982).

Roueché, *Performers and Partisans*   C. Roueché, *Performers and Partisans at Aphrodisias in the Roman and Late Roman Period, Journal of Roman Studies*, Monograph 6 (London 1993).

INDEX OF PEOPLE AND PLACES

INDEX OF SUBJECTS